soo fariista
COME SIT DOWN

Soo fariista
COME SIT DOWN
A Somali American Cookbook

· · · · · · · · · ·

Wariyaa
SOMALI YOUTH IN MUSEUMS

· · · · · · · · · ·

MINNESOTA
HISTORICAL
SOCIETY PRESS

Photos on pages 7 (left, middle), 8 (left, middle), 9, 41, 47 (bottom), 117: Andrea Ellen Reed. Photos on pages 7 (right), 8 (right), 47 (top, middle), 71, 77 (top), 127, 131, 181: Wariyaa program. Photos on pages 27, 35, 57, 143, 153, 157, 167, 175: Anne Levin, Elena Everson, Susan Everson. All other photos by James Castle.

www.mnhspress.org

The Minnesota Historical Society Press is a member of the Association of University Presses.

Manufactured in the United States of America

10 9 8 7 6 5 4 3 2 1

∞ The paper used in this publication meets the minimum requirements of the American National Standard for Information Sciences—Permanence for Printed Library Materials, ANSI Z39.48-1984.

International Standard Book Number

ISBN: 978-1-68134-085-2 (paper)

Library of Congress Cataloging-in-Publication Data

Names: Wariyaa: Somali Youth in Museums.

Title: Soo fariista : come sit down, Somali American cookbook
/ Wariyaa: Somali Youth in Museums.

Description: St. Paul, MN : Minnesota Historical Society Press, [2018] | Includes index.

Identifiers: LCCN 2018009905 | ISBN 9781681340852 (paper : alk. paper)

Subjects: LCSH: Cooking, Somali. | Cooking—Minnesota—Saint Paul Area. | Somali American—Social life and customs—Minnesota—Saint Paul Area. | LCGFT: Cookbooks.

Classification: LCC TX725.S58 S66 2018 | DDC 641.596773—dc23

LC record available at https://lccn.loc.gov/2018009905

Ergo toban habeen soo dhaxdoo, timid halkaan joogo

Tuldo geela in aan gowracaad, igu taqaaneene

Gacantaan tashiishiga aqoon, sow la tebimaayo.

foreword

For Somalis, food is how we share ourselves, how we care for our communities, and where we show our values. One of the ways we demonstrate the love every Somali puts into holding our community together is through food.

We may call to mind the image of a Somali nomad: temporary home built on the wide plain, sheltered by acacia trees, a herd of camels walking in from the bush and goats grazing nearby. Another family might appear over the hill, walking to their next location. That family would need a place to stay. Without hesitation, the hosts bring out food for their guests. Camel milk, porridge with fruits and honey, beans and corn, and meat. They preserve all the leftovers, stocking up big containers of dried meat, fruit, and butter. Even if times are tight for a family, they will always keep a container of preserved food on hand. They never know when a guest may appear at their door, and guests get served first.

Historians have written about the ways Somalis passionately share food with their guests. The Moroccan traveler and scholar Muhammad ibn Battuta visited Somalia in the year 1331 and received generous welcome from his hosts. Ibn Battuta sailed from Zeila to Mogadishu and described in detail the meals he was served—rice with butter, sauces and stews of meat and vegetables, banana cooked in milk, sour milk with pickled lemon, pickled chiles with vinegar and salt, ginger, and mangoes.

Whether in a village or a big city, this sharing of food is a common part of culture for all Somalis. Preparing food for guests, and preserving food for future guests, is an important way we enact our values of hospitality, compassion, generosity, and interconnectedness. We each know that we might be the ones wandering in the bush tomorrow, that we might have just gotten off a plane from another country, and one day we'll need some extra help. Today we share what we have with you, because we know what it feels like to be in your position.

I am thrilled by this project because these young people are growing up with the culture that their parents carried. For these young people, food is a tool to touch their history and their identity. When those of us from older generations talk about our community's history and culture, youth can get an idea, but when they cook the food they can actually touch it. They can hold their culture in hand. They can taste it. It means a lot more than just learning or listening to a story.

It seems to me that these days fewer and fewer young people know how to cook. It's easy for us to get the things we need without preparing them, and we take that convenience for granted. (Of course, when I was a teenager, I didn't know how to cook, either!) These youth, though, have learned how to cook, how to prepare their food, how to get all the ingredients they need. They all know that they have really *done* something. One day they will be able to cook their food without depending on their parents. What an impression these youth will make: not only are they building skills, becoming independent, and cooking for themselves, but they are cooking their cultural food.

These young people can motivate the rest of their generation. This project will encourage other youth, who will see their peers cooking and want to learn. By learning how to prepare a meal—not just snacks or a sample, but a full meal they can present for guests—these young people are learning skills that they will take with them. I imagine some of them saying, "Hey, Mom, don't worry. I'll cook the food today." One day, we will see all of today's youth depending on themselves, carrying on their family's well-being, and looking after each other.

Many of our families came to the United States through war or struggle. As a consequence, many young people have not been able to learn from their families the way many of us did in the past. They may not have enough time to learn from their parents, or their parents may not be able to teach them, because they have many other struggles once they are here in the States. This is a special opportunity because these youth also can share their culture with neighbors who may not know about it. Here in Minnesota, youth grow up making friends with and in community with people from different roots. They have a unique opening to meet with their friends, cook them saabuuse, canjeelo, or malawax, and also taste their friends' cultural traditions. Imagine: each of these young people serving in their own way as an ambassador of their culture.

Now these youth will take that example. When a guest comes to them, they will be able to cook them a meal. Or if they do not have anything to cook, they can easily make a cup of tea. If a group of people comes to visit, these youth will represent their family and step into the role of serving their guests. I imagine these students having a friend come to their home—they will start to make them food right away. And that's how the culture will spread from one child to another, from one student to another, from one family to the next, and on and on. No matter what type of food they cook, it will be cultural food because it will be part of the web of traditions we share.

Osman Mohamed Ali, founder and executive director, The Somali Museum of Minnesota

For more on hosting guests in Somali culture, see Maxamed Cabdiraxmaan Jaamac "Luggooyo," "Marti-gelinta iyo Marti-soorka Soomaalida": http://www.dharaaro.com/index.php/culture-and-arts/culture/16-marti-gelinta-iyo-marti-soorka-soomaalida.

For more on Muhammad ibn Battuta, see Said Hamdun and Noel King, *Ibn Battuta in Black Africa* (Princeton and New York: Markus-Wiener Publishing, Inc., 1994).

Soo fariista
COME SIT DOWN

introduction

Wariyaa: Somali Youth in Museums was a yearlong project for Somali high school students to learn about the opportunities a museum provides for communities and how to preserve their own ethnic heritage. The Somali language was scripted only recently, in 1972, prompting debates of the written forms of some words. Some may say *wariyaa* means "Hey you!" or "Hey, you're in trouble!" However, the students translated *wariyaa* to mean "journalist."

Over the course of this project, we became investigators of our own culture and what it means to be Somali. *Soo Fariista / Come Sit Down* is our report. We see our people becoming entrepreneurs, opening restaurants and clothing shops. We have hopes to go to college and reclaim the degrees our parents left behind—or to travel new paths. While others may see our blue flags and our storefronts as foreign, we know that they represent what it means to be Somali. Specifically, we know that to be Somali in Minnesota means embracing our past along with our future—a future brightened by traditional poetry and spoken word and with achievements in school and beyond.

Minnesota has a longstanding tradition of welcoming refugees and immigrants. Because of this supportive climate, Minneapolis is home to the largest population of Somali immigrants in the United States, estimated in the 2015 census at 57,000. Somali communities are located in, most famously, the Cedar-Riverside neighborhood of Minneapolis, also known as "Little Mogadishu," as well as in St. Cloud, in Wilmington, in St. Paul, and even right next door.

Stereotypes persist; reporting in the media has amplified the challenges of seamless inclusion into neighborhoods where we seek to make our homes. More than a decade ago, al-Shabab was recruiting youth to defend Somali communities against Ethiopian invasion, viewing Islamic militant control of Mogadishu as a threat to Somalia's security. In 2006, twenty to twenty-five Somali youth from Minnesota left the United States to join al-Shabab. Years later, new pressures with the Islamic State presented opportunities for Somali youth to travel abroad, and Minneapolis made international headlines again in April 2015 when six Somali youth trying to leave for Syria were arrested by the FBI. This narrative has plagued our news cycles and placed harmful stereotypes on our communities.

The students of Wariyaa believe it is our job to combat those stereotypes. And what better way than to eat together and share stories?

For nine months, we met weekly at the Mill City Museum in Minneapolis. At first, it was difficult to put into words what food, culture, adaptation, and innovation meant for us. We were all new to each other, but through food we were able to find a common language. In the beginning stages of the program, we participated in lessons prepared by museums and other authorities to discuss how different cultures are represented in the classroom. Sometimes it was difficult to understand that, in trying to tell others' stories, even well-intentioned people got it wrong. It was empowering to realize that we are our own experts, even though society often tells us that we're "just kids."

Many immigrants have come before us: British, French, Swedish, Polish, Latinx, Hmong. The Somali community may be the newest in Minnesota, but there are more similarities than differences among all of us. Yes, we might say *malawax* instead of *tortilla*. We might say *shaah* or *chai* or *tea*. But, really, we are all learning how to speak to each other through culture.

Through food, we learn a shared language: one of heart, one of camaraderie, one of innovation.

Over those nine months, we collaborated. We visited museum collections, viewed exhibits, and heard our stories—sometimes for the first time. We baked, cooked, fried, and learned together. We laughed at our failures—which, through teamwork, eventually developed into our greatest triumphs. We struggled to make sense of recipes with missing information, to navigate the ever-present "just a pinch" measurement system, to assess the authenticity of the recipes with our palates.

Wariyaa students comprise a small group of Somali culture and identities. While we do not pretend to represent the community in total—just as no small group can speak for the whole—we do embody the diverse nature of the Somali diaspora. We speak *af Somaali*, Amharic, Arabic, and English. Sometimes we feel more comfortable in Somali, sometimes in English. We were born in Kenya, Ethiopia, Somalia, and Syria. Some of us have never been to Somalia, prompting the question: What makes us Somali, then?

Every week we explored this question. We are Somali because we say we are. Because our parents say we are. We eat pizza, xalwo, and suqaar. And now we even know how to make these dishes ourselves. The foods we eat have no borders. What makes us Somali is not whether we were born or lived in Somalia. It's not because we celebrate Eid al-Fitr or Thanksgiving. It's because *we are Somali*.

As with all cultures, many of our foods have specific stories and traditions associated with them. Alongside these recipes, we share cultural stories and our own recollections. You may find a common thread in these tales: grandma's food is always the best; foods found outside your culture might be "weird"; writing down your own knowledge is *hard*.

This book seeks to advocate for and empower everyone to see culture as an evolving process, one that balances immigrant narratives with assimilation pressures from the dominant culture. You will hear about our stories, our teachings, and our mistakes. We are part of the fabric of Minnesota, just as are all those who call Minnesota their home.

student profiles

The Wariyaa: Somali Youth in Museums program started as a conversation about how to create a space of learning for some of Minnesota's newest residents. Engaging with community members to discuss the community's needs was the first step. The program's specific intention was to serve the Somali community, not to dictate assumed needs from an outsider's perspective.

Those conversations uncovered a desire for Somali youth to learn their own history and take ownership over their own narrative. One approach was through food; it was important to realize that much of the kitchen wisdom is held by women of other generations. Yet the stories that came out of this program are intertwined with history. One cannot eat Somali spaghetti without understanding that the Italian colonizers brought pasta with them, or jabaati without remembering that the British brought Indian cuisine with them—and at the same time appreciate that Somalis incorporated their own spices and techniques into these dishes. And as Somali culture expands across the globe, we students realized we had our own stories to tell.

Many of us had not been in the kitchen at all, and some were the sole cooks of their family. But all of us felt the need to educate others and extend a helping hand to those who may see us as different or need a starting place to find commonality. Food is the language of the people, and just as it brought us together, we hope it brings us all together.

The recipes collected here were found in various ways: from online sources (and there aren't many!), from our families and community members, as well as from our own memories. By assembling and developing these recipes, we hope to inspire others to write down their own recipes and help teach this history to the next generation.

From September 2016 to May 2017, we met at Mill City Museum in Minneapolis, Minnesota. The result, *Soo Fariista / Come Sit Down*, is an invitation to get to know us through our stories about our lives, our families, and our kitchens.

abdirahman

I was born in Damascus, Syria, in 2001. I live with my mom, dad, and brother in Roseville, Minnesota. I came to Minnesota in January 2007, when I was five years old. I go to school at Higher Ground Academy, where I am in the eleventh grade.

abdikarim

I am from Africa and I was born in Qabribayax. When I was there I used to go to school until fifth grade. I came to the United States in 2014. It was not like Somalia at all! I live in Minneapolis now. After I finish high school, I would like to be a teacher in Africa because they need my help the most. I want to teach English and math.

abdiwahid

I was born and raised throughout most of my life in Johannesburg, South Africa. At the age of twelve, I moved to the United States. I first landed in Columbus, Ohio, where I stayed for six months and learned how to read. I then moved to Minneapolis. I enjoy playing basketball for fun and am in the chess club. I am currently in school at South High School.

asha

I am from Kenya, and my family are Somali. We were all born in Somalia. When I was in Somalia, I never went to school. My siblings and I moved to Kenya for two and a half years. My mom came to the United States in 2010, and we followed her. I love sports, especially badminton and soccer. I live in Minneapolis, Minnesota, now.

hamse

I live in Minneapolis, Minnesota, and go to South High School. When I was in Africa, I used to play a lot of soccer. When I came to Minnesota, I played soccer, but then discovered basketball. In the future, I want to return to Somalia and help the poor with what I am capable of doing.

hamdi

I was born in the Jomo Kenyatta Hospital in Nairobi, Kenya. By 1999, my family had arrived in Minneapolis, Minnesota. I am one of seven children; I have two brothers and four sisters. I live in South St. Paul and am finishing my high school career doing PSEO [Postsecondary Enrollment Options] at St. Paul College. Now as an eleventh grader I am still trying to better myself and looking to find new things.

hoda

I'm from Ethiopia. I live with my family. I have eight siblings: four boys and four girls. We have lived in the United States for two years, starting in Massachusetts. I miss Ethiopia and my grandma and all my friends. I like to do my homework, read books, help people, and play with my friends. I am in eleventh grade at South High School in Minneapolis. I want to become a math teacher.

hamze

I am from Somalia; I was born in Mogadishu. I have been in the United States for two years, and my dad still lives in Somalia. I go to South High School. I have good teachers right now. I started eighth grade when I came to Minnesota. I want to be a doctor.

naima

I'm from Ethiopia. I live with my family. We are seven kids; I have four brothers and two sisters. I came to Texas first in 2012, and then we moved to Minnesota because our cousin told us it was a better place. I want to go to Augsburg College to study psychology and work to help my family be a better family.

somali culture

Islamic practices have been deeply embedded in the Somali culture since the seventh century. Some practices related to food and gathering include eating with your right hand, saying *bismillah* (in the name of god) before eating, and not consuming alcohol or pork.

Historically, Somalia's most important export has been livestock, followed by bananas, which grow abundantly in the region. Bananas are a food staple and an iconic side paired with Somali meals. Bananas were highly exported under colonial rule, but after Somalia gained independence the country began to export sugar, livestock, fish, sesame, and other products.

Many Somalis have a deep love for the arts. In fact, Somalia is regarded as the "Nation of the Poets." Composing literature, reciting poetry, storytelling, dancing, and singing are favorite pastimes. The Somali literary tradition consists of oral stories dating back to precolonial times. Somalia did not have an official written language until the 1970s; thus, Somalis relied heavily on their elders to tell stories of their past.

Clan structures link Somali families to each other. Clans are not specific ethnic groups but rather a unit made up of different families, distinguished by region and name. Some clans are so big that they are divided into sub-clans. Clan structures were especially important during nomadic times. Some clans were pastoralists, raising sheep and goats, camels and cattle, and others were more coastal, fishing for sustenance. Families traded with each other or married into other clans to form ties that enhanced their chances for survival.

somali history

Somalia is a land of nomads, animal herders who have traveled throughout the Horn of Africa for centuries. Now many are forced to leave their homeland to escape war and terrorism. The undercurrent of constant political and cultural change is ever present in Somali food, culture, and history. Somali merchants of the third and second millennium BCE interacted with Indian, Roman, Egyptian, Greek, and Persian traders, bringing in such goods as cinnamon by way of Sri Lanka and Indonesia and such culinary traditions as flatbreads like jabaati and roti by way of India.

During a time that was hailed as the Age of Discovery, also known as the Scramble for Africa, multiple European powers invaded various African nations, plundering them for resources and waging wars against their people. In East Africa, the Portuguese tried to conquer parts of Somalia and its neighboring countries. At the start of the sixteenth century, Somali and Abyssinian forces clashed, leading to a partial takeover of Ethiopia by Somalis to protect the Islamic city-state there. Then Portuguese invaders arrived to colonize Ethiopia, thwarting the Somali advance. By the 1580s, the two countries were deeply embattled. The Portuguese military pillaged the city-states of Kilwa, Mombasa, Malindi, Pate, and Lamu. With support from the Ottoman Empire—shared cultural practices and a devotion to Islam unified the two groups—Somali forces recaptured many cities and eventually the Portuguese were driven out. Throughout the sixteenth and seventeenth centuries the Ottoman Empire remained a close ally and economic partner to Somalia.

In 1884, when German chancellor Otto von Bismarck convened the Berlin Conference, also known as the Congo Conference, fourteen European countries partitioned the African continent based on natural resources and access to human labor—in the presence of the Ethiopian king and without consulting with any other African leaders. Somalia, with its arid landscape and highly mobile nomadic people, was a less desirable parcel. Italy, late to the conference, took on Somalia as a means to improve economic conditions at home.

In the 1920s, Benito Mussolini sought to expand his fascist empire, ordering the Italian military to invade Somalia and overthrow sultanates, forcing them out of their homelands. Mussolini and the Italian empire colonized Somalia, renaming it *La Grande Somalia*. On May 9, 1936, Mussolini officially proclaimed the creation of the Italian Empire and named his "new" land, encompassing Ethiopia, Eritrea, and Italian Somaliland, "Italian East Africa." During World War II, numerous Somali men were forced to train in the Italian Royal Corps of Colonial Troops, and by 1940 there were roughly twenty-two thousand Italians living in Somalia.

During this time a small portion of modern-day northern Somalia was occupied by the British Empire. North of the British colony was French Somaliland. By the end of World War II, British armed forces had conquered Italian Somaliland, but in 1950 the United Nations granted Italy trusteeship over Italian Somaliland under the watchful eye of the newly formed Somali Youth League, among other political groups. Fourteen years later, on July 1, 1960, the two territories, British and Italian, were reunited to form the Somali Republic. French Somaliland never joined its homeland: after the colony required a bailout, a failed referendum led to formation of the state of Djibouti in 1977.

the somali diaspora

The results of European conquest are still felt throughout Somali communities and within Somali food traditions. Spaghetti, curry, and bananas (first brought by the Italians) are only small parts of the colonial legacy. Unstable economic and cultural divides in the wake of the British and Italian Empires pointed the newly independent Somali Republic toward civil war. After decades of internal fighting and struggles to reunite fractured clans and reestablish tribal affiliations—and then a wave of nationalism that brought British Somaliland and Italian Somaliland to unity under one flag in 1960—a military dictatorship was formed under Major General Mohamed Siad Barre.

Barre headed the Somali Revolutionary Socialist Party, or SRSP. However, once in power, Barre rebranded his party as the Supreme Revolutionary Council. Despite assassination attempts, Barre's regime remained in power from 1980 to 1991, when it finally collapsed. In 1992 the United Nations, with the aid of the US military, invaded Somalia under a supposed peacekeeping mission. However, numerous battles broke out between the peacekeepers and the Somali military. The UN retreated in 1995.

In 2000 Abdiqasim Salad Hassan was elected president of the newly established Transitional National Government. Despite the semblance of stability and a reduction in fighting nationwide, there was still massive civil unrest. In 2012 the Federal Government of Somalia became the country's first permanent central government since 1991. During that decade, an estimated 300,000 to 500,000 people had died and upwards of one million were displaced.

In addition to hundreds of thousands of Somali people fleeing their homeland during the civil war, the fighting and unrest birthed terrorist groups, most notably al-Shabab. The militant group purportedly joined forces with al-Qaeda, and their violent actions further contributed to the immense number of Somali refugees and displaced people.

Between 1990 and 2015, the number of Somalis born in Somalia but living elsewhere more than doubled from 850,000 to two million, the majority of them refugees. Today there are over a million Somali refugees worldwide. Roughly 900,000 Somali refugees live in neighboring countries such as Kenya, Ethiopia, Djibouti, and Yemen. An estimated 280,000 Somali immigrants and refugees live in Europe, and about 150,000 live in the United States. Of those, a large portion have settled in Minnesota, with a concentration in the Twin Cities of Minneapolis and St. Paul. As of 2013 there were an estimated 25,000 Somalis living in Minnesota, with that number projected to increase.

While the American metaphors of melting pot or tossed salad are apt for this nation of immigrants, food can also bridge the diaspora, creating commonalities across distance. In short, food is a unifying factor for culture.

somalis in minnesota

The earliest Somali immigrants to Minnesota arrived in the 1960s. Most sought education or business opportunities. However, when the civil war broke out the United States saw an increase in the number of Somali migrants. With a small Somali population already established in the Twin Cities, refugees found their way there through voluntary agencies that helped them settle into their new home. Today, the Cedar-Riverside neighborhood of Minneapolis is a bustling Somali community, with numerous Somali-owned restaurants, bakeries, and shops. However, it is increasingly common to find Islamic community centers, mosques, and Somali businesses scattered throughout the Twin Cities metropolitan area.

Minnesota is home to a flourishing Somali community. The integration of Somali immigrants and refugees into the fabric of the state and its culture is hard to ignore. Often public signs and informational graphics employ English, Spanish, and Somali, widening accessibility to growing populations. The number of Somali students in Minnesota schools and the state university system continues to expand. The influx of Somalis to the Twin Cities has brought huge economic benefits: Somalis own more than six hundred businesses in the area and contribute upwards of $400 million in purchasing power. Furthermore, the state can boast the first and only Somali American in US politics: Ilhan Omar, a Somali refugee, was elected to the Minnesota House of Representatives in 2016.

The Somali community thrives as its members adjust to the frozen north, but they also recognize the history that makes them unique. The recipes found here are a mixture of traditional Somali culture, colonial influence, and modern adaptation. All represent the community as it was and as it is. The students learned how to cook thinking about their own history, but they also learned that they are empowered to define that history and make it their own.

1

holiday dishes

Holidays bring huge gatherings: cooking large meals and eating as a family are essential components of joyous celebrations. Abundant stews, plentiful breads, and delicate desserts are incorporated into holiday and religious gatherings. Many of these dishes require multiple hands to achieve.*

The two major holidays in Islam are Eid al-Fitr and Eid al-Adha. Both involve large feasts. Eid al-Fitr is celebrated after the holy month of Ramadan, which is observed as the ninth month of the Islamic calendar. During Ramadan, Muslims worldwide fast from dawn to dusk and join with family and friends to break their fast after sundown. Eid al-Fitr, known as the "feast of breaking the fast," is celebrated over the course of three days. Eid al-Adha, the "feast of the sacrifice," celebrates Abraham's willingness to sacrifice his son to Allah. Before Abraham could do so, however, a sheep was put in his son's place. In remembrance, an animal—a lamb, goat, or sheep, depending on the region—is sacrificed during Eid al-Adha and the meat is divided into three parts, shared among family, friends, and the poor. In Somalia, common foods during Eid al-Fitr and Eid al-Adha include xalwo, shushumow, saabuuse, oodkac, and buskud.

Other important celebrations with corresponding large gatherings include birthdays, anniversaries, Somali Independence Day, baby showers, funerals, and, most elaborately, weddings. Sometimes weddings are divided by gender, but it is increasingly common for all guests to attend in the same place. Somali weddings are extravagant parties at which entire extended families join myriad friends and neighbors and all dress with a vibrant flourish.

*We regularly see holiday dishes on restaurant menus, suggesting widespread availability and ease of preparation. However, our time in the kitchen proved this interpretation to be illusory. These dishes are meant to be shared with friends and family—and that includes the work of making them. We hope you invite people into your home to help you with these delicious recipes!

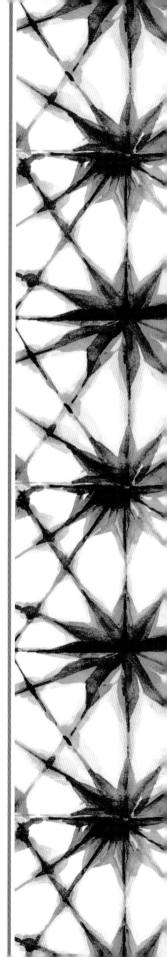

Saabuuse (sambusas) are ubiquitous at Somali parties and are also served as appetizers at restaurants. Hot sauce (Shidni, page 118, or Basbaas, page 120) generally accompanies them. As a group, we assumed that since saabuuse appear at family gatherings and holidays as well as in restaurants they must be easy to make. After our first attempt, though, Abdirahman said, "I have so much more respect for what my mom does in the kitchen." This recipe is for the wrappers; recipes for fillings are on the following pages.

saabuuse wrappers SERVES 10+

3 ¼ cups all-purpose flour, divided

¼ teaspoon salt

1 ¼ cups lukewarm water, divided

3 cups vegetable oil for frying, plus more for brushing

hot sauce for serving

Mix 3 cups flour and salt in a bowl, then slowly knead in 1 cup water. Continue to knead the dough for 5 to 10 minutes, until it is pliable and there are no lumps. Form the dough into a ball and divide into 8 equal portions. Roll each into a ball, coat with oil, and set aside.

Heat a skillet on medium-low heat. On a floured surface, working with 2 balls at a time, roll each into a 5-inch circle. Brush one with oil and align the other on top. Use a rolling pin to roll out the stacked rounds to 10 to 11 inches in diameter. Cut into 4 triangular wedges.

Place 1 piece dough on the warm skillet and heat until dry, about 30 seconds, then flip and dry the other side; be sure not to cook too long. Remove and let cool slightly, then slowly separate the two layers. Place on a plate and cover with a towel. Repeat steps until all dough has been prepared.

In a small bowl, mix remaining ¼ cup flour and ¼ cup water to make a smooth paste. Take one saabuuse wrapper and fold it, oiled side out, into a cone shape, sealing the sides with flour paste. Place 2 tablespoons of filling in the cone and fold the outside in to make a pocket. (See photos on page 25.) Bring the top of the wrapper down to make a triangle, and seal with flour paste. Pinch the edges to completely seal. Set aside, and continue filling the rest of the saabuuse.

Heat oil in a skillet, and cook the saabuuse until they are golden brown, about 5 minutes each side. Or heat oil in a deep fryer and cook for 5 to 10 minutes. Remove from oil and drain on a paper towel–lined plate. Serve warm, with hot sauce.

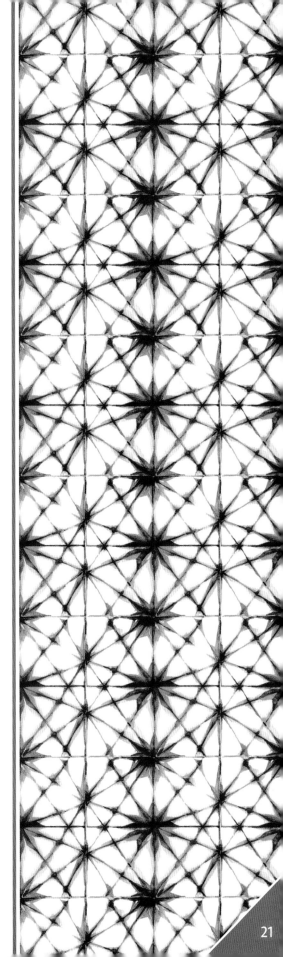

beef saabuuse filling

SERVES 10+

1 pound ground beef or lamb

2 teaspoons ground coriander

2 teaspoons ground cumin

2 teaspoons ground cardamom

2 teaspoons curry powder

salt and pepper to taste

2 tablespoons vegetable oil

3 green onions, minced

1 small yellow or white onion, minced

2 serrano chiles, minced, or to taste

1 clove garlic, minced

2 tablespoons minced fresh cilantro*

In a large bowl, mix the meat with the spices (coriander, cumin, cardamom, curry powder, salt, pepper). In a skillet over medium heat, heat oil and cook the meat until browned. Stir in the onions, chiles, garlic, and cilantro and continue to cook until meat is tender, about 20 minutes. Let cool to room temperature.

Refer to the Saabuuse Wrappers recipe (page 20) to finish this dish.

⟨ *Waxannu barannay* ⟩ WE LEARNED

*In our discussion of ingredients, we realized that cilantro and coriander are different names for the same plant. In the United States, *cilantro* usually refers to the fresh leaves, while *coriander* refers to the seeds. None of us could remember the Somali word for this plant. But it made sense when Asha grabbed the cilantro leaves to add them in.

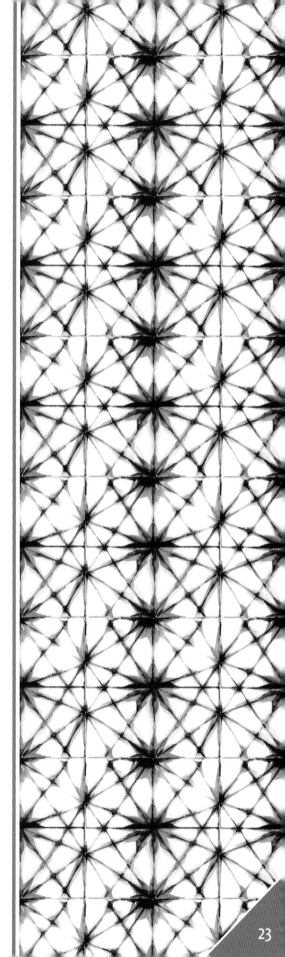

lamb saabuuse filling

SERVES 10+

2 tablespoons vegetable oil

1 pound ground or diced lamb

½ onion, chopped

2 cloves garlic, minced

1 tomato, chopped (about 1 cup)

2 serrano chiles, chopped, or to taste

1 teaspoon Xawaash (page 142), or substitute cumin

chopped fresh cilantro to taste

salt

Heat a large pan over medium-high heat. Drizzle oil into pan and add lamb. Cook, stirring to break up meat, until the lamb is lightly browned. Add onions and garlic. Cook, stirring, until softened, about 5 minutes. Add tomato and cook until liquid has evaporated. Add chiles, xawaash, cilantro, and salt to taste. Cook until the pan is dry, about 30 minutes (a wet filling will make the saabuuse fall apart). Let cool to room temperature.

Refer to the Saabuuse Wrappers recipe (page 20) to finish this dish.

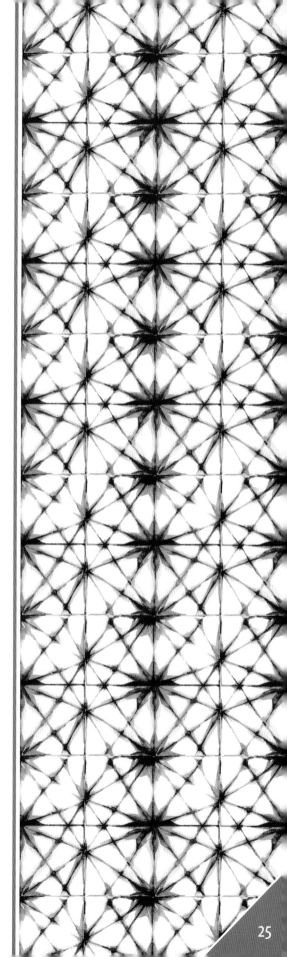

vegetarian saabuuse filling

SERVES 10+

½ cup green lentils, rinsed and drained

1 ½ cups vegetable broth

2 tablespoons vegetable oil

½ onion, chopped

1 clove garlic, minced

2 serrano chiles, minced, or to taste

2 teaspoons curry powder

1 teaspoon ground cardamom

½ teaspoon ground cumin

salt to taste*

In a saucepan, stir together lentils and broth. Bring to a boil, reduce heat to simmer, and cook, partially covered, until liquid is completely absorbed and lentils are tender.

Heat oil in a skillet set over medium heat, then add onions, and cook, stirring, until tender. Add garlic and chiles and cook until softened, 15 to 20 minutes. Stir in cooked lentils, curry powder, cardamom, cumin, and salt and cook for 5 minutes, until heated through. Let cool to room temperature.

Refer to the Saabuuse Wrappers recipe (page 20) to finish this dish.

⟨ *Waxannu barannay* ⟩ WE LEARNED

*According to Asha, "salt to taste" is not an optional suggestion. You should add at least ¼ teaspoon.

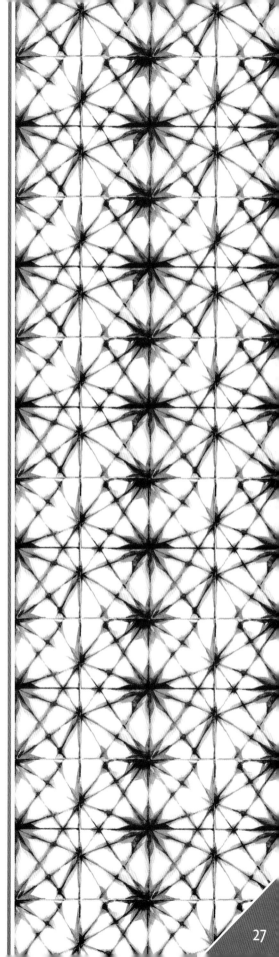

A culinary tradition born of nomadic life in Somali culture, oodkac, or preserved meat, sustained long-distance travelers with necessary protein. However, with the abundance of meat in American culture, this dish is now saved for special occasions. Serve with Canjeelo (page 48) or Sabaayad (page 52).

oodkac/muqmad
JERKY-STYLE MEAT; SERVES 6

2 pounds beef or goat, cut into ½-inch cubes

1 teaspoon salt

about 3 cups canola oil

16 tablespoons (2 sticks) butter

½ onion, diced

2 cloves garlic, minced

½ teaspoon ground cardamom

In a large saucepan set over medium heat, cook meat for approximately 5 minutes, until well browned; drain. Add salt and enough canola oil to cover. Fry for 20 minutes, stirring continuously. When meat has dried to the consistency of beef jerky, cool to room temperature and remove to an airtight storage container. The dried meat will keep for 2 weeks or longer.

In a separate pan, melt the butter over medium heat and cook the onions, garlic, and cardamom until the onion is translucent, about 10 to 15 minutes. Pour mixture through a strainer to remove solids. To serve, drizzle fragrant butter over meat.

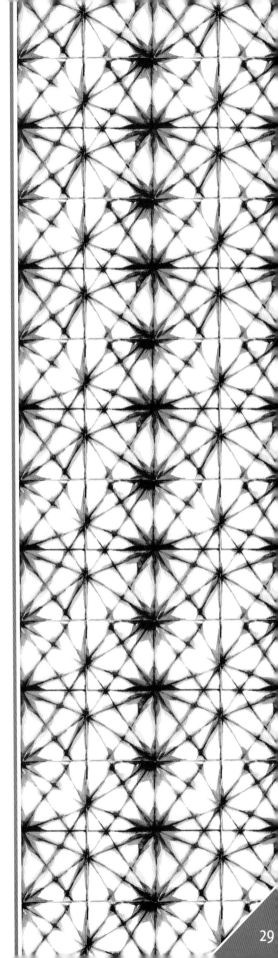

"My mom remembers that her parents would buy xalwo and lock it in a cabinet. This was because her and her sisters used to overeat it, and their parents had to do something about it. They knew where their mom kept the key, so they used to sneak some out when she was sleeping." —Abdirahman

This addictive, sweet dessert is often found at celebrations and is served with Buskud (page 32)—or on its own, if you can't wait for the cookies!

somali xalwo/halwad
SWEET SPREAD; SERVES 10+

2 cups granulated sugar

2 cups packed brown sugar

4 cups water, divided

1 cup cornstarch

1 cup vegetable oil

2 teaspoons ground cardamom

1 teaspoon ground cloves

In a saucepan over high heat, bring the sugars and 3 cups water to a boil. In a bowl, mix cornstarch and remaining 1 cup water until dissolved.* Stir the mixture into the boiling sugar syrup. Cook over medium heat for about 30 minutes, stirring frequently. As the mixture thickens, begin adding oil (be careful: if the mixture is too hot, the oil will spatter), stirring in more when the mixture sticks to the bottom of the pan. Once the mixture begins to pull away from the sides of the pan, stir in cardamom and cloves. Remove from heat and pour onto a parchment paper–lined baking sheet. Let cool, then cut and serve.

⟨ *Waxannu barannay* ⟩ WE LEARNED

*Dissolve the cornstarch or it will form clumps. The clumps do not take away from the taste, but they do make you look like an amateur.

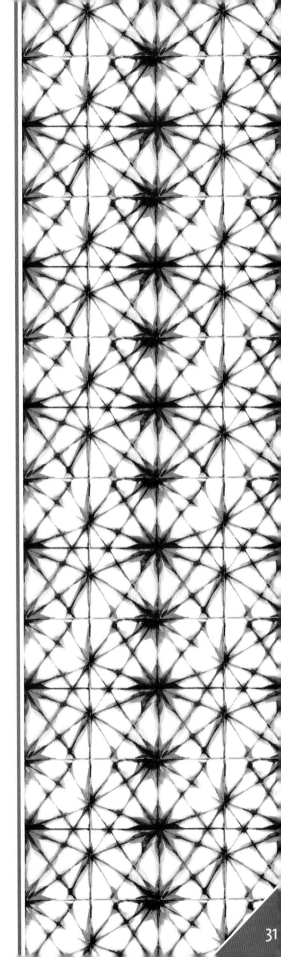

These cookies are served with Halwad (page 30) spread on top like jelly. The cardamom of the biscuits cuts through the sweetness of the halwad. Or substitute Cardamom Cookies (page 34) for a truly Minnesota-immigrant experience: Swedish and Somali desserts!

buskud

SOMALI BISCUITS;* MAKES ABOUT 60 BISCUITS

16 tablespoons (2 sticks) butter

1 cup sugar

3 eggs, beaten

2 cups self-rising flour

1 cup all-purpose flour

2 teaspoons ground cardamom

Preheat oven to 350 degrees and line baking sheets with parchment paper. In a saucepan, melt butter and stir in sugar. Cool slightly, then stir in beaten eggs, combining thoroughly. In a large bowl, sift together flours and cardamom. Gradually add in butter-sugar-egg mixture, stirring until batter no longer sticks to the side of the bowl. On a floured surface, roll out to ½-inch thickness and cut into desired shapes. Place on prepared baking sheets and bake 10 to 12 minutes, until golden brown.

〈 *Waxannu barannay* 〉 WE LEARNED

*In true colonial fashion, we debated whether to call these biscuits or cookies. An argument for the latter: they are soft and sweet like a cookie.

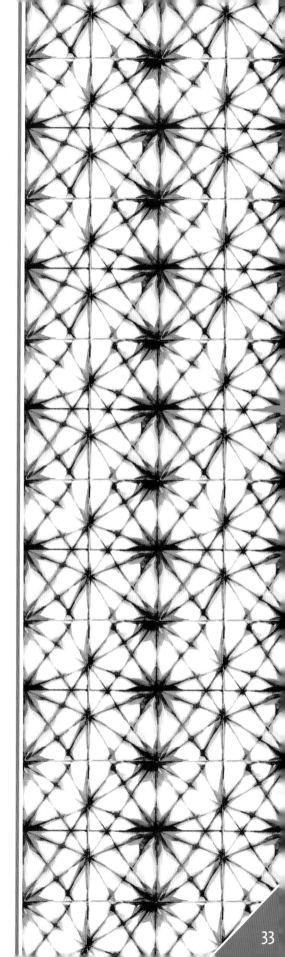

Some say that Vikings found cardamom a thousand years ago in northern India and introduced it into Scandinavia, where its flavor remains popular today. This highly scented spice has a variety of uses depending on the region: the Near East and Scandinavia consume half the world's cardamom. In Sweden, it is more widely used than cinnamon.

cardamom cookies

MAKES ABOUT 36 COOKIES

8 tablespoons (1 stick) butter, softened

½ cup sugar

2 egg yolks or 2 tablespoons egg substitute

1 cup all-purpose flour

½ teaspoon baking powder

½ teaspoon ground cinnamon

½ teaspoon ground cardamom

Heat oven to 375 degrees and line baking sheets with parchment paper. In a large bowl, beat butter until creamy. Stir in sugar until smooth. Add egg yolks and mix well. Add flour, baking powder, cinnamon, and cardamom, stirring until all the flour is mixed in. Using spoon or hands drop ¾-inch balls of dough at least 1 inch apart onto prepared baking sheets. Press lightly to flatten. Bake for 10 to 12 minutes, until golden.

⟨ *Waxannu barannay* ⟩ WE LEARNED

Interpreters at Mill City Museum in Minneapolis use this recipe to discuss community influences in this very diverse city. These cookies were the first dish we cooked together—and the first time we understood that food truly is the language we have in common. And as we discussed what to call the ingredients, we realized how ubiquitous cardamom is in Somali cuisine.

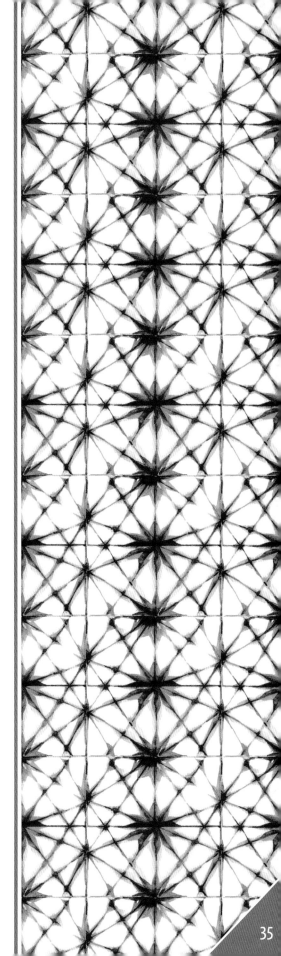

luqaimat

SWEET FRITTERS; MAKES ABOUT 30 FRITTERS

2 cups all-purpose flour

1 tablespoon instant yeast

1 tablespoon yogurt

2 ½ cups warm water, divided

1 tablespoon vegetable oil, plus more for frying

2 cups sugar

juice of 1 lemon

sesame seeds, optional

In a large mixing bowl, stir together flour, yeast, yogurt, 1 ½ cups water, and 1 tablespoon oil into a thick batter. Set in a warm place to rise, about 30 minutes. A humid, enclosed space that is at least 80 degrees or an oven with a proofing setting will work. When the dough has doubled in size and irregular bubbles are visible, it is ready to use.

Meanwhile, stir together remaining 1 cup water, sugar, and lemon juice in a large saucepan and boil until the syrup is sticky, about 5 minutes. Set aside.

Heat oil in a deep fryer or a deep pan over medium heat. Test the oil by dropping in a bit of batter: when the batter floats up quickly, the heat is right. Portion batter into tablespoon-size balls and drop a few at a time gently into the oil. Turn the balls constantly to ensure even cooking. When lightly golden, remove them from the pan and drain on paper towels. Drop into syrup, stirring gently to coat. Roll the syrupy balls in sesame seeds for an extra hit of flavor.

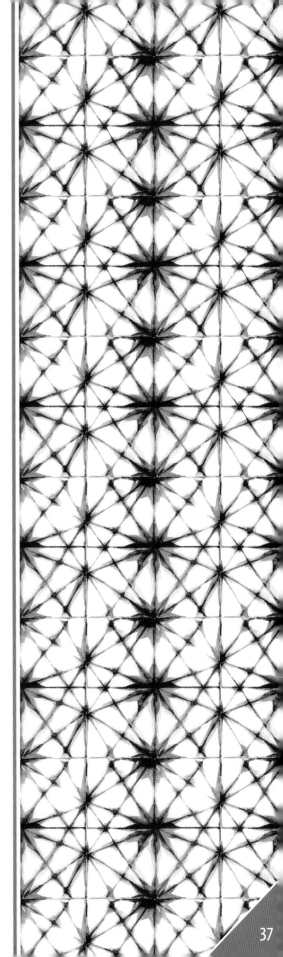

This crispy, sweet pastry is often served during holidays and celebrations. The dough is shaped into small balls and then curled in a manner similar to Italian gnocchi. The method of rolling and shaping shushumow is part of the Italian colonial legacy, but these desserts are uniquely Somali.

shushumow

CRYSTALLIZED PASTRY SHELLS; MAKES 30 SHELLS

1 ½ cups all-purpose flour

½ cup plus 3 tablespoons sugar, divided

½ teaspoon baking powder

¼ teaspoon salt

⅓ cup canola oil, plus 2 cups for frying

1 egg

½ cup water, divided

¼ teaspoon ground cardamom, optional

In a large bowl, stir together flour, 3 tablespoons sugar, baking powder, salt, ⅓ cup oil, and egg.* Gradually stir in ¼ cup water to make a soft, elastic dough. Mix for about 4 to 5 minutes, then set aside for about 30 minutes.

Form the dough into about 30 (1-inch) balls. Shape one at a time by pressing each piece flat with the back of a fork. Lift the closest edge and curl the dough forward into a spiral shape.

Heat 2 cups oil over medium heat. Fry the shushumow in the oil, turning to brown evenly. Drain finished shushumow on paper towel–lined plate.

In a medium saucepan stir together remaining ½ cup sugar, remaining ¼ cup water, and cardamom (if using) and let mixture come to a boil. Simmer for a couple of minutes, then remove from heat. Add all the shushumow to the pan, stirring gently to coat evenly. Remove shushumow to a plate and let the sugar crystalize.

⟨ *Waxannu barannay* ⟩ WE LEARNED

*We did not often have access to stand mixers, food processors, or blenders during our program. Many times the students reminded each other that their families wouldn't have had those tools either. Good thing the Wariyaa students have strong arms for stirring.

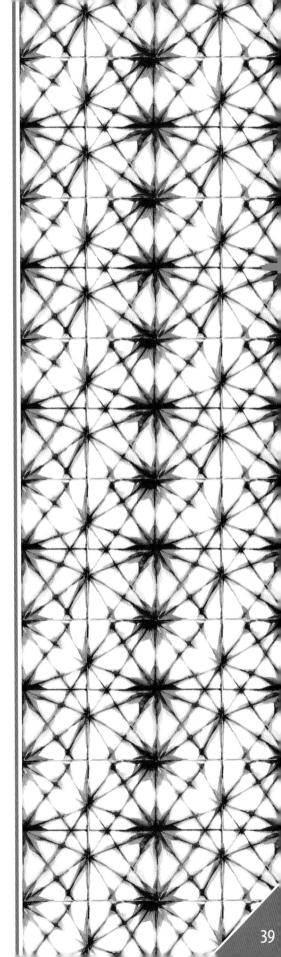

The first time Hamdi's family celebrated Thanksgiving they also celebrated their new country by adding to their Somali traditions. She and her sisters were proud of the cake they made and will remember it as their own Thanksgiving specialty.

pineapple upside-down cake

SERVES 10

4 tablespoons (½ stick) butter, melted

⅔ cup packed brown sugar

1 (14.5-ounce) can pineapple rings, drained

Betty Crocker Super Moist Favorites Yellow Cake Mix*

Heat oven to 350 degrees. Coat interior of a 9x13–inch pan with melted butter, spreading along sides to prevent the cake from sticking. Sprinkle brown sugar evenly over the bottom of the pan. Arrange pineapple slices over brown sugar. Prepare cake mix according to package instructions and pour evenly over the pineapple slices. Bake according to package instructions. Invert finished cake over a serving platter and remove from pan. Spoon any brown sugar mixture remaining in pan evenly over the cake and serve warm.

⟨ *Waxannu barannay* ⟩ WE LEARNED

*Use your own cake recipe if you prefer. On the day we made the cake, we were in the baking lab at the Mill City Museum, formerly the home of the Washburn-Crosby Company, which launched the baking persona Betty Crocker. Using one of "her" recipes seemed just right.

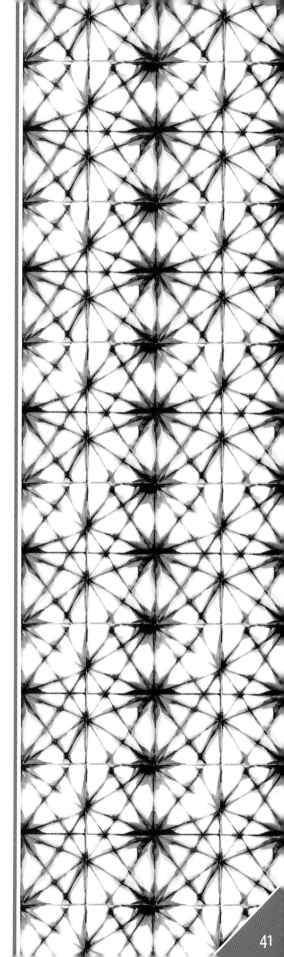

breads

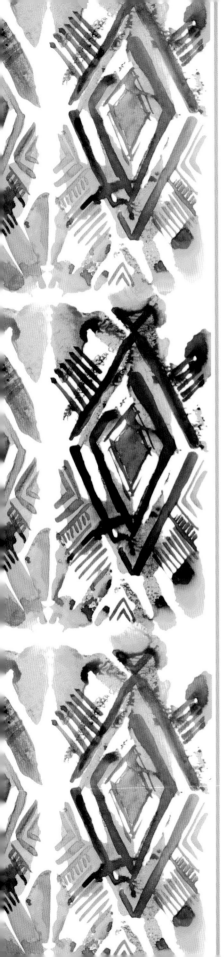

All cultures share a love of bread. Bread holds various textures and sizes and is put to many uses, but its presence at our meals unifies generations and civilizations. Regional influences—Ethiopian, Kenyan, or Somali—determine the types of bread on the family table.

For Somalis, bread is used for sandwiches, as a side dish, and at times as an eating utensil. Flatbreads are the most common type of bread found throughout Somalia. Often made in a wood-burning stone oven or on a crêpe skillet, flatbreads are incorporated into numerous dishes. Canjeelo is common at breakfast, paired with honey and ghee or butter and sugar and served with Somali tea or coffee. Malawax, roti, and sabaayad, along with canjeelo, appear at lunch and dinner, served with curries, stews, and meats. Sometimes onions or sesame oil will be added for a savory flavor.

"Alarm clocks aren't what wakes me up in the morning; instead, my mind was conditioned by the smell of malawax sizzling on top of the stove. Some of the best memories come from times when my family ate breakfast together. When I was younger my mom would always be in the kitchen making the household's favorite breakfast food: malawax. We would all instantly wake up knowing who was in the kitchen and what they were making just from that familiar, delightful smell that permeated through the house. When my mom finished making the traditional Somali pancake she would serve it with a stew or suqaar and Somali tea. She would limit everyone to two or three pancakes, until everyone ate. When everyone ate she would double anyone's plate. The best part of this memory is sitting with my mom as she told us funny stories about her childhood or week. I loved listening to what my mom had to say while stuffing my face! Those mornings were filled with laughter, and the mornings and eating breakfast was considered one of our most valuable family times." —Hamdi

malawax

SOMALI SWEET FLATBREAD; SERVES 4

3 cups milk

4 eggs

2 cups all-purpose flour

½ cup plus 2 tablespoons sugar

¼ teaspoon salt

1 tablespoon ground cardamom

vegetable oil for cooking

honey or syrup for serving

In a large bowl, stir together milk, eggs, flour, sugar, salt, and cardamom, mixing well. Heat 2 tablespoons oil on a griddle over medium heat.* Ladle ¼ cup batter onto griddle. To create the traditional shape, pour the batter into the center of the pan and then move the ladle in concentric circles outward. Cook for 2 minutes or until bubbles start to form. Flip and continue cooking until both sides are golden. Continue with remaining batter, adding more oil as needed. Serve hot with honey.

⟨ *Waxannu barannay* ⟩ WE LEARNED

By the time we finished testing this recipe, we realized it was completely different from where we had started. One day, we didn't have any honey, but we had a gift of real maple syrup from a Menominee friend, which worked just as well.

*The traditional Somali pan, bir canjeelo, is made of cast iron. Somali women often carried these heavy pans in the diaspora. A crêpe pan or griddle can be used instead.

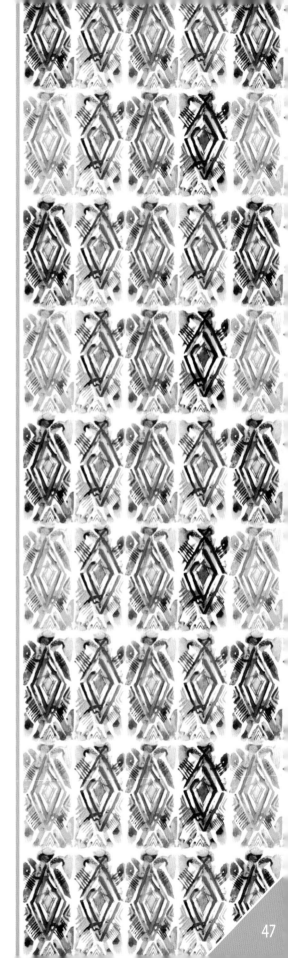

Pronounced *ahn-jel-lo*, not to be mistaken for Ethiopian injera, this flatbread is used to soak up savory sauces and stews. The technique is the same as for Malawax (page 46), but the flavor is savory.

canjeelo
FLATBREAD; SERVES 6

2 cups self-rising flour

2 ⅔ cups warm water

2 tablespoons vegetable oil, plus more for cooking

¼ teaspoon salt

In a large bowl, stir together flour, water, oil, and salt until smooth; let sit for 15 minutes. Heat a pan or griddle over high heat and lightly oil surface. Ladle ¼ cup batter onto griddle, spread as shown at right, and cook until the top is bubbly and the bottom is golden brown. Flip and continue cooking until both sides are golden.

One day in the kitchen, we realized we did not have any of the ingredients for traditional canjeelo, but one of our helpers, Maryan, brought a health-conscious approach and improvisation to this adaptation.

quick canjeelo
SERVES 6

2 cups quick-cooking oats

½ cup Bisquick

½ teaspoon ground cinnamon

pinch salt

1 ½ cups warm water

1 egg

vegetable oil for cooking

In a large bowl, stir together oats, Bisquick, cinnamon, salt, water, and egg until batter is smooth with no lumps. Heat a pan or griddle over high heat and lightly oil surface. To create the traditional shape, use a ladle to pour ¼ cup of the batter into the center of the pan, and then use the ladle to make concentric circles outward. The bread is done when the top is bubbly and the bottom is golden brown.

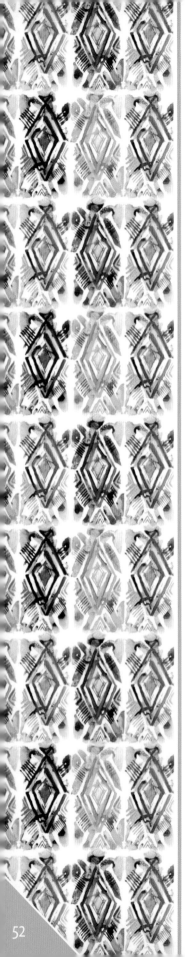

Similar to Indian *paratha*, this bread efficiently soaks up delicious sauces.

To make square sabaayad, fold the edges of the circle into the center.

sabaayad

SOMALI FLATBREAD; MAKES 8 BREADS

2 cups all-purpose flour

1 cup whole-wheat flour (called *atta* in Indian grocery stores)

½ teaspoon salt

**2 tablespoons vegetable oil or ghee
(clarified butter), plus more for cooking**

about 1 cup water

In a large bowl, stir together flours and salt. Slowly add 2 tablespoons oil and mix in thoroughly. Gradually add in the water, kneading the dough until firm and elastic. Set aside for at least 30 minutes.

Divide the dough into 8 portions. On a lightly floured surface, roll out each portion into a circle. Spread 1 teaspoon oil on each circle and rub gently all over the surface.

Heat a skillet or griddle over medium heat. Add 1 dough circle to the pan, greased side up, and let it cook for a minute or so. When it starts to puff, flip the sabaayad and immediately spread a teaspoon of oil on top. Use a spatula to press down the bread all around, which will make it puff more evenly. When it is browned, flip again and finish cooking on the first side. Remove from heat and place on a plate. Continue with the remaining sabaayad. Serve hot.

coconut-filled sabaayad

SOMALI FLATBREAD; MAKES 8 BREADS

2 cups all-purpose flour

1 cup whole-wheat flour

1 teaspoon salt

1 cup water

2 tablespoons vegetable oil or ghee (clarified butter), plus more for frying

shredded coconut and sugar to taste

In a large bowl, stir together flours and salt. Slowly add water to mixture and knead by hand until smooth. Cover and let rise for 30 minutes.

Divide dough into 8 portions. On a lightly floured surface, roll each portion into a thin, flat circle. Brush each piece with oil and sprinkle with coconut and sugar.* Fold the edges to meet the center to make a square. Roll out each piece flat.

Heat 2 tablespoons oil in a medium saucepan. Working in batches, cook sabaayads until golden brown, turning once. Remove to a paper towel–lined plate. Serve warm.

〈 *Waxannu barannay* 〉 WE LEARNED

*Fresh coconuts are challenging to find in the decidedly non-tropical state of Minnesota, so we often used desiccated coconut from the baking aisle. Choose whatever version is readily available to you. If desiccated, be sure to hydrate it first.

Made using a process similar to Canjeelo (page 48), these savory pancakes are a wonderful vegan and gluten-free accompaniment to a vegetarian dish like Lentil Curry (page 100) or Spinach and Chickpea Curry (page 102).

chickpea pancakes

MAKES 4–6 PANCAKES

½ teaspoon cumin seeds

1 cup chickpea (garbanzo) flour

¼ teaspoon chile powder or red pepper flakes

½ teaspoon ground turmeric (use fresh for a stronger flavor)

½ teaspoon salt

1 cup water

1 tablespoon olive or coconut oil

Add cumin seeds to a small skillet over medium heat. Toast cumin for 30 seconds to 1 minute until fragrant. Remove from heat. In a large bowl, stir together flour, cumin, chile powder, turmeric, and salt. Slowly add water, blending or whisking until smooth. Heat a skillet or griddle over medium heat and add oil. Ladle about ¼ cup batter onto the pan and use ladle to spread. Cook for about 3 minutes or until golden brown, then flip and cook for another 2 to 3 minutes. Repeat with remaining batter, adding oil to the pan as needed.

British influence on Somali cuisine is visible in the blending of foods from other colonized places. Somali intuition saw these dishes as complementary to their own culture. Chapati, a traditional bread from India, was encountered by refugees in Kenya and remade as jabaati.

jabaati/chapati
MAKES 10

1 cup whole-wheat flour

1 cup all-purpose flour

1 teaspoon salt

2 tablespoons olive oil, plus more for cooking

about ¾ cup hot water

In a large bowl, stir together flours and salt. Stir in the oil and enough water to make a soft dough that is elastic but not sticky. Knead the dough on a lightly floured surface until smooth. Divide into 10 portions.* Roll each piece into a ball and let rest for a few minutes. Use a floured rolling pin to roll out the dough balls until very thin, like a tortilla.

Heat a skillet over medium heat until hot; add a drizzle of olive oil. When the pan starts smoking, add a dough round. Cook until the underside has brown spots, about 30 seconds, then flip and cook on the other side. Repeat with remaining dough.

⟨ *Waxannu barannay* ⟩ WE LEARNED

*Divide the dough into smaller portions to make mini jabaati to accompany a delicious suqaar.

58

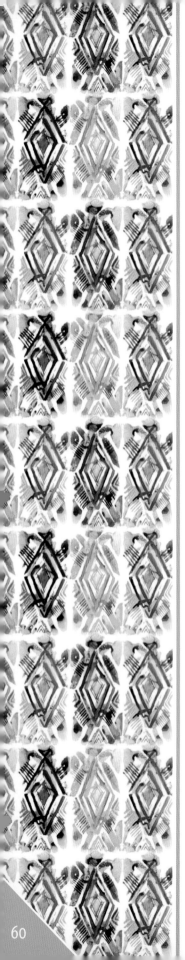

These corn flatbreads were traditionally cooked by throwing the dough onto the interior roof of a clay oven. However, this technique would make a mess of our modern ovens, so the recipe has been adapted to today's home kitchen. We savored this dish, but in truth most families do not make this one at home: muufo is most commonly found in restaurants.

muufo/kidaar
CORN FLATBREAD; MAKES 15

2 cups white corn flour

1½ cups all-purpose flour

¼ cup sugar

1 teaspoon salt

1 teaspoon instant yeast

2 cups warm water

In a large bowl, stir together flours, sugar, salt, and yeast until combined. Add water and knead until dough is elastic. Cover and let rise for 1 hour.

Heat a skillet that has a lid over medium heat. Moisten your hands in a bowl of water and shape a fistful of dough. Form the dough into a round shape and place it in the middle of the pan. Flatten the dough with a spoon or, if you're brave, the back of your hand. Cover and cook for 3 minutes. Flip and cook, uncovered, for another minute. Repeat with remaining dough.

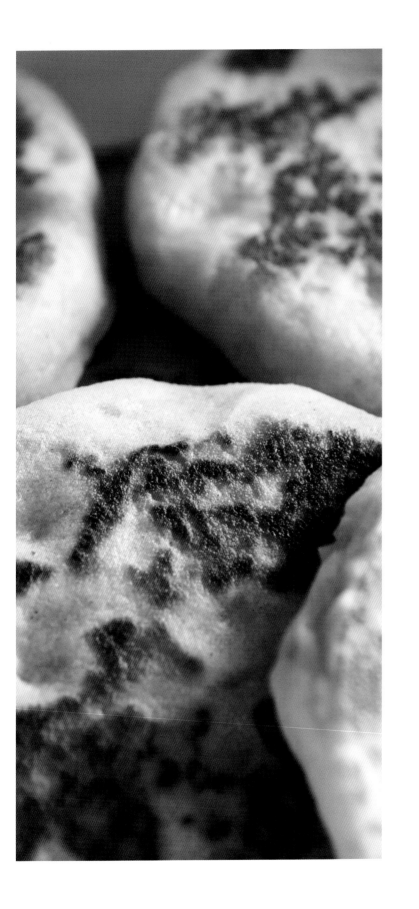

meat

A nomadic and herding society naturally develops a cuisine that celebrates meats of all sorts. As preservation of meat was an important aspect of survival in ancient Somalia, oodkac, a specially prepared sun-dried meat that would last a long time, became a popular staple. Halal practices of meat processing are also a vital part of Somali food culture. Animals must be slaughtered in accordance with Islamic tradition in a process called gawrac. Under this ritual, the animal is to be killed swiftly by slicing the carotid artery and must be slaughtered facing the holy site of the Kaaba in Mecca while an Islamic prayer is uttered. In addition, halal practice forbids the consumption of pork, blood, or alcoholic beverages.

Somalia's coastline on the Red Sea and the Indian Ocean also brings an abundance of seafood to the Somali table. Salmon, tuna, lobster, and shrimp are just some of many products coastal Somalis catch for their own consumption or to ship to more arid regions.

This rich, savory dish is best served with Sabaayad (page 52), Jabaati (page 58), or another flatbread. The recipe is flexible: add vegetables or spices as desired when you combine the chicken and the sauce.

suugo curry
BUTTER CHICKEN CURRY; SERVES 4

2 pounds skinless, boneless chicken, cut into bite-size pieces

¼ cup white vinegar

1 tablespoon olive oil

2 red onions, diced

4 small tomatoes, diced (about 2 cups)

2 tablespoons chopped fresh cilantro

1 clove garlic, peeled

8 tablespoons (1 stick) butter, divided

1 teaspoon ground turmeric

1 teaspoon salt or to taste

½ cup heavy cream

Toss chicken with vinegar, stirring to coat. Heat a skillet over medium-high heat and add olive oil. Add chicken and cook, stirring, until browned and dry. Remove from heat.

Make the curry sauce by combining onions, tomatoes, cilantro, and garlic in bowl of a blender and blending for 1 minute.

Melt 4 tablespoons butter in a large saucepan. Add the cooked chicken, curry sauce, and turmeric. Heat to boiling, stirring frequently. Add salt, cream, and remaining 4 tablespoons butter, stirring well. Cover, reduce heat to medium low, and cook for about 20 minutes.

Suqaar, or sautéed meat, is an important staple in Somali cuisine. This recipe can be prepared with beef, goat, or lamb as well. Serve with rice, Sabaayad (page 52), or bread.

chicken suqaar
SERVES 4

2 teaspoons vegetable oil

1 pound skinless, boneless chicken, cubed

1 teaspoon chile powder

1 teaspoon ground cumin

salt and pepper to taste

1 small onion, diced

2 teaspoons lemon juice

1 teaspoon white vinegar

1 teaspoon chopped fresh cilantro

1 summer squash or zucchini, sliced

Heat oil in a skillet over high heat and add the chicken, cooking until browned. Stir in chile powder,* cumin, salt, and pepper. Stir in onions and cook until softened. Stir in lemon juice, vinegar, and cilantro. Add squash and cook until tender, about 15 minutes.

⟨ *Waxannu barannay* ⟩ WE LEARNED

*While these recipes call for specific spices, we often improvised along the way—and you should do the same. Many of the dishes are meant to be flavorful, not spicy. Just beware of the serrano chiles.

This dish, tested in our early kitchen days, taught us to double-check that someone had set a timer. We knew the chicken was done when it started to smell amazing, "just like my kitchen!" Serve with rice or French Fries (page 116).

digaag duban
SPICY BAKED CHICKEN; SERVES 4–6

1 teaspoon salt or to taste

1 teaspoon pepper

1 teaspoon ground cumin

½ teaspoon ground coriander

½ teaspoon ground cardamom

juice of 1 lemon

2–3 tablespoons olive oil

2 pounds chicken legs (or drummies)

Stir together salt, pepper, cumin, coriander, and cardamom; mix in lemon juice and 2 tablespoons oil. Coat chicken thoroughly with mixture, adding more oil as necessary. Set aside for at least 30 minutes or refrigerate overnight.

Heat oven to 350 degrees. Place chicken on a baking tray and bake for 25 to 35 minutes, until pieces reach an internal temperature of 165 degrees.

Suugo, meaning sauce, is similar to stews found in traditional American cookbooks. Suugo is best soaked up with Canjeelo (page 48). This suugo is also good with rice or Sabaayad (page 52).

lamb & potato suugo

SERVES 4

¼ cup vegetable oil

about ½ pound lamb, cubed

1 onion, chopped

1 teaspoon garlic powder

1 teaspoon ground coriander

1 large potato, peeled and cubed

2 tablespoons tomato paste

½ cup water

1 teaspoon ground turmeric

1 teaspoon curry powder

salt

Heat oil in a large skillet over medium-high heat and cook lamb until lightly browned. Add onions and cook until browned, about 3 minutes. Add garlic, coriander, and potatoes and cook, stirring, for 1 minute. Stir in tomato paste, water, turmeric, and curry powder. Cook on low heat until the sauce thickens and the potatoes are tender, about 30 minutes. Add more water if the sauce seems dry. Season with salt to taste and serve.

Traditionally, mishkaki are made as grilled meat kabobs. However, when we tested this recipe, we may have forgotten the skewers and didn't have a grill (oops!). We adapted the technique to bake them in the oven for a crispier texture. Alternatively, to make the traditional skewered version, add ¼ cup of bread crumbs to the mixture, form portions on to skewers, and grill or fry for 5 minutes per side. Either way: serve with rice.

mishkaki
MEATBALLS; SERVES 8–10

2 pounds ground chicken, lamb, or beef

1 egg

½ cup bread crumbs

1 small onion, minced

2 cloves garlic, finely minced

2 teaspoons curry powder

1 ½ teaspoons lime juice

2 serrano chiles, minced

½ cup minced fresh cilantro*

¼ teaspoon salt

In a large mixing bowl, stir together all ingredients. Refrigerate for 1 hour or overnight.

Preheat oven to 425 degrees and lightly grease a baking sheet. Roll mixture into 1-inch balls. Brown briefly in a greased skillet over medium heat, then arrange on prepared baking sheet. Bake for 25 minutes or until golden brown.

⟨ *Waxannu barannay* ⟩ WE LEARNED

*Asha is one of our best cooks: she says she can "just feel it" when a dish is ready. However, we discovered over our months together that she didn't like cilantro and often left it out. Eventually, we grew wise to her tastes and started adding it in on the side.

During our time cooking, beef was a go-to ingredient because it was readily available. However, we also explored options at farmers' markets, local Somali butchers (halal markets), as well as local grocery stores.

beef suqaar

BEEF SAUTÉ; SERVES 6–8

2 tablespoons olive oil

1 ½ pounds beef, cubed

1 small onion, diced

3 cloves garlic, minced

1 green bell pepper, diced

1 ½ cups beef broth

2 beef bouillon cubes

3 carrots, peeled and sliced

2 potatoes, cubed

rice for serving

½ bunch fresh cilantro, chopped

1 serrano chile, diced, optional

Drizzle oil into a large saucepan over medium heat and cook the beef until browned. Stir in the onions, garlic, and pepper and cook until softened, stirring frequently. Stir in the broth, bouillon cubes, carrots, and potatoes and simmer until tender, about 30 minutes. Then stir frequently until the liquid thickens into a gravy. Add more broth or water as needed to keep meat from drying out. Serve with rice, garnished with cilantro and serrano chile (if using).

This version of spaghetti is decidedly Somali because of the unique spice blend. The spice racks in Somali kitchens are always well loved.*

baasto

PASTA; SERVES 6–8

4 cloves garlic, minced

1 teaspoon ground cumin

1 teaspoon salt

1 teaspoon ground turmeric

1 teaspoon paprika

1 teaspoon Italian seasoning

½ teaspoon pepper

¼ cup olive oil

1 pound lean ground beef

1 onion, diced

1 large potato, peeled and cubed

2 carrots, peeled and diced

2 (14-ounce) cans diced tomatoes

2 tablespoons chopped fresh cilantro

1 (16-ounce) package angel hair pasta

In a small bowl, stir together garlic, cumin, salt, turmeric, paprika, Italian seasoning, and pepper. Heat oil in a large saucepan over medium heat. Add ground beef, breaking it up with a spoon, and cook until browned, about 5 minutes, stirring frequently. Stir in half of the seasoning mix. Add onions and cook until softened, about 5 minutes. Add potato and carrots. Cook, covered, stirring occasionally, until slightly softened, about 5 minutes. Stir in tomatoes and bring sauce to a boil. Reduce heat to medium-low. Stir in cilantro and remaining seasoning mix. Simmer, stirring occasionally, until flavors combine, 30 to 40 minutes. Add a little water if the sauce seems too thick.

Meanwhile, bring a large pot of lightly salted water to a boil. Add pasta and cook until al dente, 4 to 5 minutes. Drain. Serve sauce over pasta.

⟨ *Waxannu barannay* ⟩ WE LEARNED

*Instead of measuring out these individual spices, substitute 2 tablespoons Xawaash (page 142).

An important component of the Somali diet, pasta (*baasto*) is just one obvious legacy of Italian colonialism.

baasto iyo hilib shiidan

PASTA BOLOGNESE; SERVES 6–8

1 (1-pound) package spaghetti

2 tablespoons olive oil

1 pound ground beef

1 onion, minced

2 cloves garlic, minced

5 ripe tomatoes, diced (about 3 cups)

3 tablespoons tomato purée

salt

small bunch fresh cilantro, chopped

Bring a large pot of salted water to a boil. Add spaghetti and cook until al dente. Drain and set aside in a serving bowl.

While the noodles are cooking,* heat olive oil in a large skillet over medium-high heat. Add beef and cook, stirring to break up meat, until browned. Add onions and garlic and cook, stirring, until softened. Add tomatoes and tomato purée and bring to a simmer, cooking for 45 to 60 minutes. Add salt to taste, pour sauce over noodles, and garnish with cilantro.

❮ *Waxannu barannay* ❯ WE LEARNED

*We learned a lot about time management. Some of us had never made pasta before, and when we made the sauce we forgot to cook the noodles ahead of time. Our lunch started a little later that day.

On a summer trip to Africa, Hamdi ate fried livers for breakfast. While this dish created controversy within our group, it was agreed that it is very Somali to eat liver—whether you like it or not.

hamdi's livers*

SERVES 6

2 tablespoons olive oil

1 onion, diced

1 green bell pepper, diced

1 pound goat or beef liver, chopped

2 chicken bouillon cubes

salt

Heat oil in a large cast-iron skillet over high heat until smoking. Add onions and green pepper and cook, stirring frequently, until softened, about 5 minutes. Add liver and bouillon cubes and cook for approximately 15 minutes, adding water if pan becomes dry. Season with salt to taste.

⟨ *Waxannu barannay* ⟩ WE LEARNED

*It was often remarked that you aren't Somali until you eat banana mashed into your rice and livers.

Somalia has a lengthy coastline, but many in the diasporic community have gone to inland places. This recipe connects the numerous geographical areas where Somalis live today.

While not typically associated with African cuisine, fish dishes are popular throughout many communities along the Red Sea and the Gulf of Aden. Serve with rice, pasta, or a simple curry.

pan-fried kingfish fillet

SERVES 4

4 (1-inch-thick) slices kingfish fillet, or substitute sea bass, mackerel, or tuna

white vinegar, optional

½ teaspoon smoked paprika

¼ teaspoon salt

¼ teaspoon pepper

juice of 1 lemon

3 tablespoons vegetable oil, divided

Rinse the kingfish fillets thoroughly and dip in vinegar (if using); pat dry. Season fish with paprika, salt, pepper, and lemon. Heat a large shallow pan over medium heat and add 1½ tablespoons oil. Shallow-fry 2 fillets skin-side down for 5 minutes, then flip and cook the other side for 5 minutes; remove to a plate. Repeat with remaining oil and fish.

malai kismayo

FRIED FISH; SERVES 4

1 tablespoon ground cumin

2 cloves garlic, crushed

juice of 1 lemon

1 tablespoon white vinegar

¼ teaspoon salt

1 (2-pound) firm-fleshed fish fillet*

olive oil for frying

Stir together cumin, garlic, lemon juice, vinegar, and salt. Rub all
over fish fillet; set on a plate and refrigerate for 30 minutes. Heat
a lightly oiled skillet over medium heat. Fry the fish for about
2 minutes or until browned. Flip and cook for another 2 minutes.
Remove the fish to a paper towel–lined plate.

〈 *Waxannu barannay* 〉 WE LEARNED

In true Minnesota fashion, we chose walleye
as our fish fillet. Halibut or cod will work, too.

sides & sauces

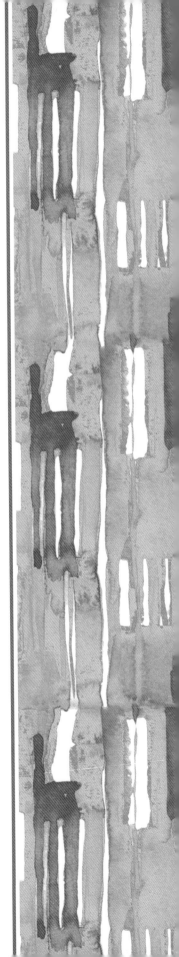

Sides and sauces are essential accompaniments to Somali dishes: any meal without some *basbaas* (hot sauces) or a *moos* (banana) is incomplete. Somali mealtime features vegetables and fruits that grow in different areas of the country, each dish highlighting complementary flavors. The Somali palate tends toward savory, but nomads would also sweeten their food with sugar, honey, and ghee.

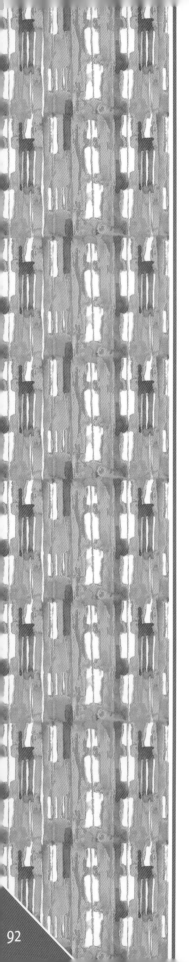

We sought out this dish when we realized vegetables were missing from our collection. Like most high school students, our group had focused on meat instead. Naima suggested using this recipe because fava beans remind her of her grandma.

shahan ful

FAVA BEANS IN SPICY TOMATO SAUCE; SERVES 6

1 tablespoon olive oil

1 large onion, minced

1 clove garlic, minced

2 teaspoons salt

1 tablespoon curry powder

1 ½ teaspoons ground cumin

1 teaspoon garlic powder

1 teaspoon ground coriander

1 teaspoon pepper

1 teaspoon paprika

1 large tomato, diced (about 1 cup)

1 tablespoon chopped fresh cilantro

juice from ½ lemon

1 (14-ounce) can fava beans, rinsed and drained*

Heat oil in a large skillet and cook onions and garlic until softened. Stir in spices (salt, curry powder, cumin, garlic powder, coriander, pepper, and paprika) and cook for 5 minutes. Stir in tomatoes, cilantro, lemon juice, and beans and cook for 10 to 15 minutes, until heated through.

〈 *Waxannu barannay* 〉 **WE LEARNED**

*If you can't find fava beans in your local grocery store, lima beans are a great substitution. Chickpeas can be used in a pinch.

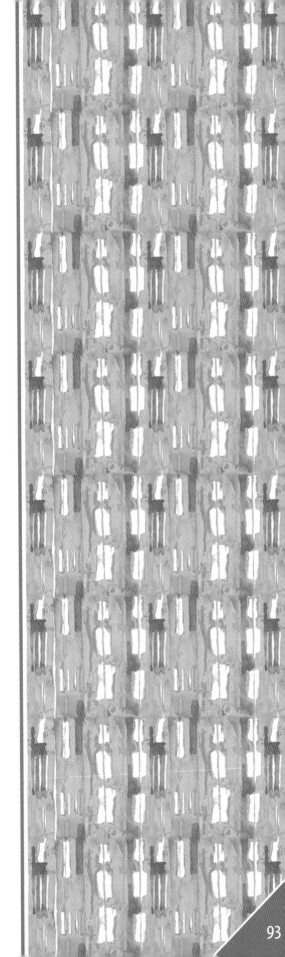

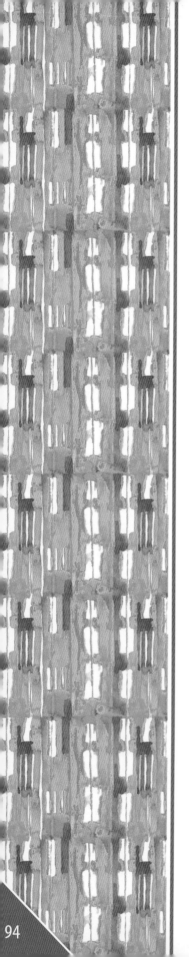

walnut & cumin lentil salad

SERVES 4–6

1 tablespoon olive oil

1 large onion, diced

2 cloves garlic, minced

1 teaspoon ground cumin

1 (15-ounce) can brown lentils, rinsed and drained, or 1 cup cooked lentils

1 tablespoon sesame oil

juice of ½ lemon

1 tablespoon white vinegar

salt and pepper

½–1 cup cherry tomatoes, halved

¼–½ cup chopped walnuts

handful chopped fresh cilantro

Heat olive oil in a large skillet over medium heat and cook onions until softened. Stir in garlic and cook for 1 minute. Add cumin and lentils, reduce heat to low, and cook for about 5 minutes. Remove from heat.

In a small bowl, stir together sesame oil, lemon juice, vinegar, a pinch of salt, and a pinch of pepper. Stir dressing into the lentils. Stir in tomatoes, walnuts, and cilantro; add salt to taste.

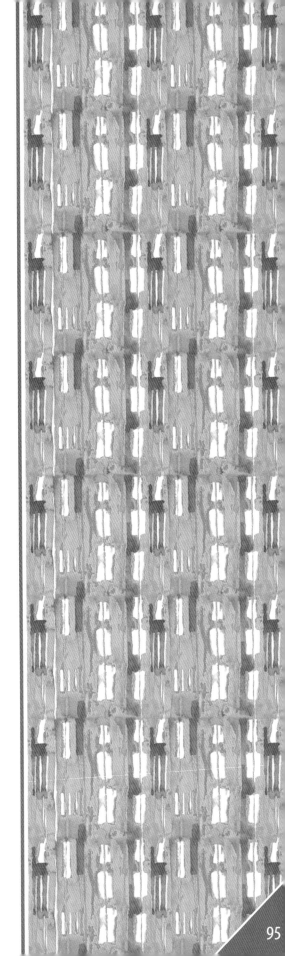

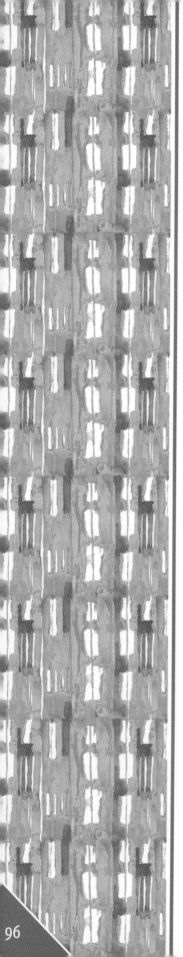

This salad with its simple dressing is a perfect side dish. We used half a red and half a green pepper for vibrant color. (And we even ate our vegetables that day!)

sweet potato & lentil salad

SERVES 6

2 medium sweet potatoes, peeled and cut into half-inch rounds

1 tablespoon olive oil

2 (15-ounce) cans lentils, rinsed and drained

1 cup cherry tomatoes, halved

1 bell pepper, diced

1 cup rocket salad leaves (arugula), or substitute other flavorful lettuce

2 tablespoons chopped fresh cilantro

1 teaspoon ground turmeric

1 teaspoon ground cumin

½ teaspoon salt

bread for serving

YOGURT & TAHINI DRESSING

juice of 1 lemon

1 red onion, cut into rings

2 cloves garlic, minced

salt

sugar

3 tablespoons thick plain yogurt

1 tablespoon tahini

Heat oven to 350 degrees. Brush the sweet potato with olive oil and place on a baking sheet. Bake until cooked through, about 10 minutes.

Make the dressing: In a small bowl, stir together lemon juice, red onion, garlic, a pinch of salt, and a pinch of sugar. Set aside for about 5 minutes; this reduces the raw onion's bite. Stir in yogurt and tahini until well blended.

In a medium bowl, stir together lentils, tomatoes, bell pepper, rocket salad leaves, cilantro, turmeric, cumin, and ½ teaspoon salt.

Spread the dressing on a large serving plate. Layer roasted sweet potatoes on dressing and pile the rest of the salad on top. Serve with some good bread.

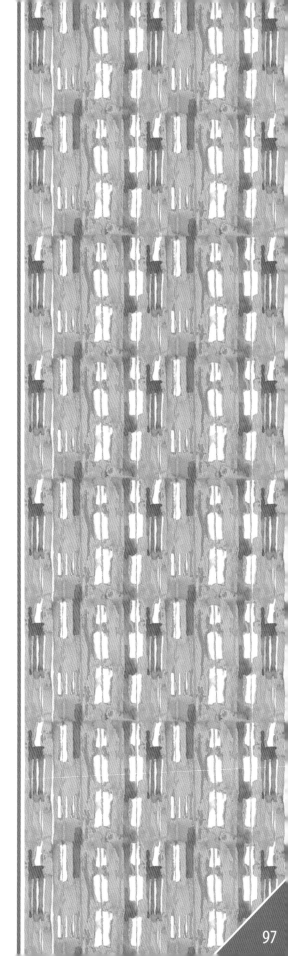

misir iyo lows

LENTILS WITH ALMONDS; SERVES 4–6

1 tablespoon olive oil

1 teaspoon mustard seeds

1 onion, diced

2 green chiles, diced, optional

1 teaspoon ground cumin

1 teaspoon ground coriander

1 teaspoon ground turmeric

2 tomatoes, diced (about 1 ½ cups)

2 cups cooked lentils, or 2 (15-ounce) cans
lentils, rinsed and drained

1 teaspoon sugar

¼ teaspoon salt

1 tablespoon tamarind paste*

small bunch fresh cilantro and/or handful
fresh fenugreek or thyme leaves

¼ cup slivered almonds

Heat oil in a medium skillet over medium heat and toast
mustard seeds. As soon as they start to pop, add the onions and
chiles (if using) and cook, stirring often, for about 2 minutes.
Stir in cumin, coriander, and turmeric and cook 1 minute. Stir
in tomatoes, lentils, sugar, salt, and tamarind paste. Cover and
cook over low heat for about 10 minutes, stirring occasionally.
Add a few tablespoons of water if the mixture seems dry. Serve,
garnished with herbs and almonds.

⟨ *Waxannu barannay* ⟩ **WE LEARNED**

*Tamarind paste can often be found in the
"ethnic" section of the grocery store, near
South Indian sauces. If you don't have access
to tamarind paste, substitute lime juice.

A flavorful, vegetarian curry option.
Best served with Canjeelo (page 48) or rice.

lentil curry

SERVES 4–6

1 tablespoon vegetable oil

½ teaspoon mustard seeds

1 onion, minced

½ teaspoon cumin seeds or ¼ teaspoon ground cumin

½ teaspoon grated ginger

½ teaspoon minced garlic

salt

juice of 1 lemon

2 (15-ounce) cans brown or green lentils, rinsed
and drained, or 2 cups cooked lentils

2 tomatoes, diced (about 1 ½ cups)

½ cup water

Heat oil in a medium skillet over medium heat and toast mustard seeds (and cumin seeds, if using). As soon as they start to pop, add onions and cook, stirring, until golden. Stir in cumin, ginger, garlic, salt, and lemon juice and cook for a minute or so. Stir in lentils, tomatoes, and water. Simmer for about 10 minutes. Season with salt to taste.

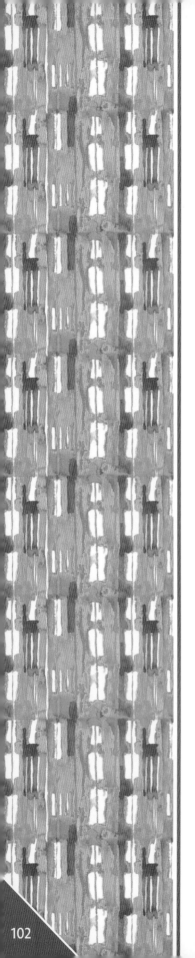

This vegan dish brings Indian flavors to the table.
Try it with Muufo (page 60) or Sabaayad (page 52).

spinach & chickpea curry

SERVES 4–6

1 tablespoon olive oil

1 large onion, minced

1 tablespoon curry powder

3 tomatoes, diced (about 2 cups)

2 cloves garlic, minced

2 green chiles, minced

4 cups lightly packed fresh spinach,
or 1 cup frozen spinach, thawed

1 cup chickpeas, soaked overnight and boiled,
or 1 (15-ounce) can chickpeas, rinsed and drained

salt

1 tablespoon chopped fresh cilantro or chives

Heat oil in a large skillet over low heat; add onions and cook slowly until deeply browned and caramelized, about 30 minutes. Stir in curry powder and cook for 2 minutes. Increase heat to medium, stir in tomatoes, garlic, and chiles and cook for about 5 minutes. Add the spinach and cook, stirring, for 5 minutes. Stir in the chickpeas and cook for 3 minutes. Season with salt to taste. Garnish with cilantro or chives.

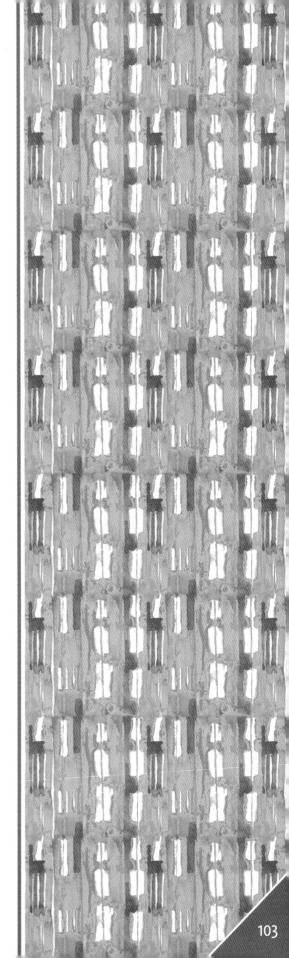

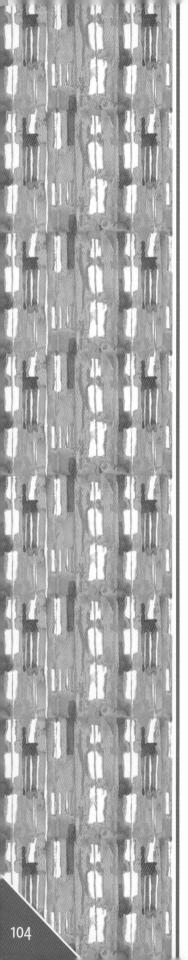

Sweet potatoes and a variety of vegetables make this one-pot dish a healthy meal all on its own, but it's also tasty with bread or served over rice.

spicy vegetable hotpot

SERVES 4–6

1 tablespoon olive oil

1 onion, minced

2 cloves garlic, minced

2 green chiles, minced, optional

1 teaspoon ground cumin

1 teaspoon ground turmeric

2 cups peeled cubed sweet potato

1 (14.5-ounce) can diced tomatoes

1 cup cooked navy or other beans,
or 1 (15-ounce) can beans, rinsed and drained

¼ teaspoon salt or to taste

1 cup water

1 cup fresh broccoli florets

½ cup fresh green beans cut into thirds

In a large saucepan with a lid, warm olive oil over medium heat and cook onions until translucent, 3 to 4 minutes. Add garlic, chiles, cumin, and turmeric and cook, stirring, for 1 minute. Add sweet potatoes, tomatoes, navy beans, salt, and water; mix well. Cover and simmer for 15 minutes over medium heat. Stir in broccoli and green beans. Simmer additional 10 minutes, uncovered, until vegetables are tender.

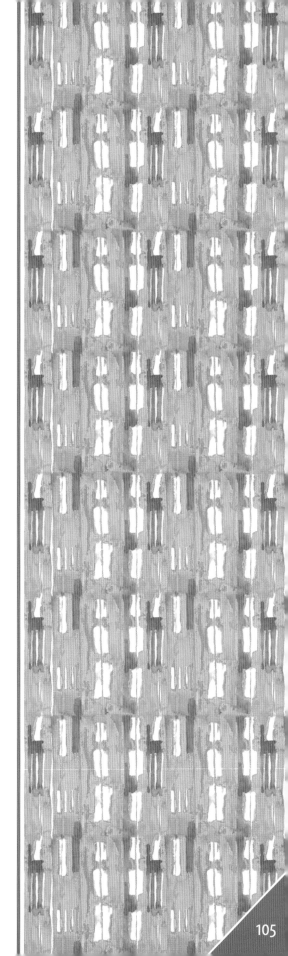

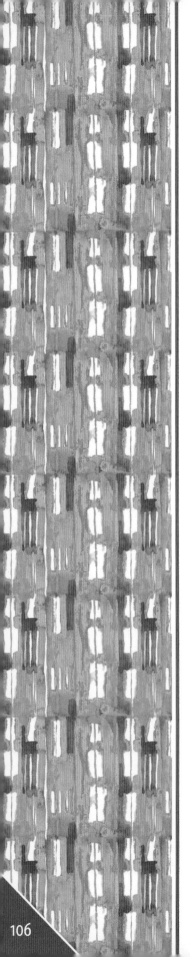

This dish relies on seasonal vegetables, which may make for a different look during Minnesota's cold winter months. Use what is fresh and local.

khudaar la shiilay
VEGETABLE STIR-FRY; SERVES 6

2 tablespoons olive oil

1 onion, chopped

1 cup chopped mixed bell peppers

1 rib celery, chopped

1 squash, pumpkin, or sweet potato, peeled and diced (about 2 cups)

2 tomatoes, diced (about 1 ½ cups)

1 cup chopped silverbeet (Swiss chard)

salt

1–2 sprigs thyme, optional

Heat oil in a large skillet over medium heat. When hot, add onions and cook, stirring, until lightly browned. Add bell peppers, celery, and squash and cook, stirring, for about 2 minutes. Add tomatoes and stir for a minute. Add silverbeet and cook, stirring often, for 3 minutes. Season with salt to taste; garnish with thyme (if using).

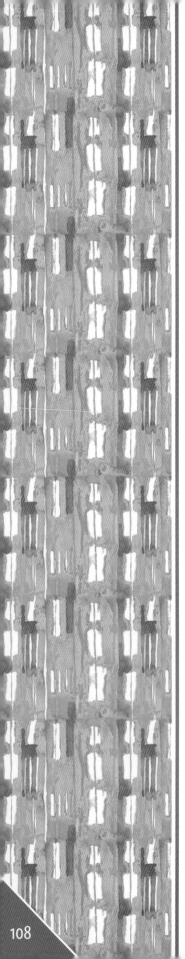

Pumpkins and squash signal the approach of
fall and winter for Minnesotans. This hearty
dish makes for a refreshing seasonal meal.

maraq bocor
PUMPKIN SOUP; SERVES 4

2 teaspoons olive oil

1 small onion, chopped

1 teaspoon ground cumin

1 cup diced pumpkin or squash

½ cup chopped mushrooms

1 small red bell pepper, chopped

2 small eggplants, cubed (about 3 cups)

2 cloves garlic, crushed

2 small tomatoes, diced (about 1 ½ cups)

1 teaspoon tomato paste

1–2 green chiles, diced

½ cup fresh cilantro leaves, plus more for garnish

1 cup water, plus more as needed

salt

Heat oil in a large saucepan and cook onions and cumin until
browned. Stir in pumpkin, mushrooms, bell pepper, eggplant,
garlic, tomatoes, tomato paste, chiles, and cilantro; cook for a
few minutes. Stir in water and salt to taste. Cook, covered, until
vegetables are tender, about 30 minutes. Check occasionally and
add water as needed.

Carefully pour hot soup into blender bowl and purée to desired
consistency. Serve garnished with cilantro.

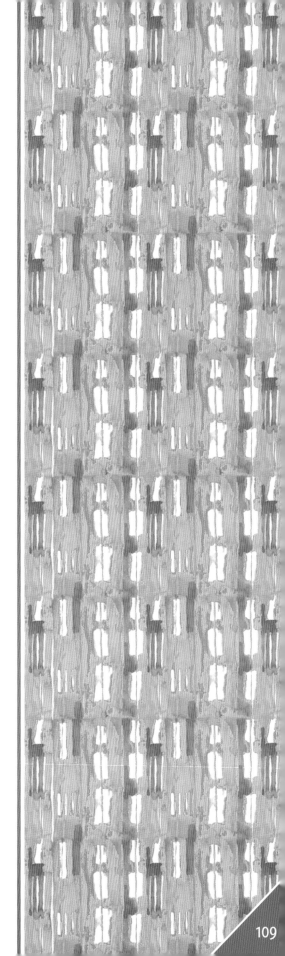

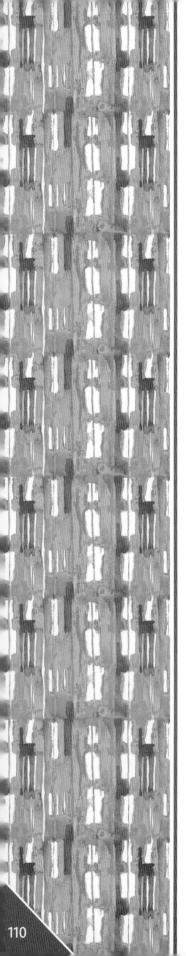

This hearty side can serve as a friendly reminder of home during the long winter months. It also makes for a flavorful vegetarian main.

kashmiri chile cabbage

SERVES 4

2 tablespoons sesame seeds

1 teaspoon cumin seeds

2 tablespoons olive oil or ghee (clarified butter)

1 large onion, diced

1 teaspoon grated ginger

1 teaspoon minced garlic

½ teaspoon ground turmeric

¼ teaspoon salt

6 Kashmiri chiles, minced, or substitute 1 tablespoon paprika plus ½ teaspoon cayenne

½ teaspoon red chile flakes or powder

2 cups chopped cabbage

In a small skillet over medium heat toast sesame and cumin seeds for about a minute or until fragrant. Remove from heat and set aside.

Heat oil a large skillet over medium heat and cook onions until translucent. Stir in ginger, garlic, turmeric, salt, Kashmiri chiles, and chile flakes and cook for a minute. Stir in the sesame seeds, cumin seeds, and cabbage and mix thoroughly. Cover and cook for about 5 minutes or until the cabbage is tender.

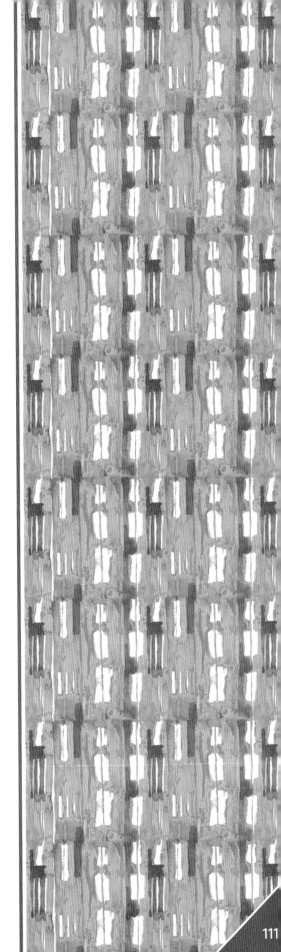

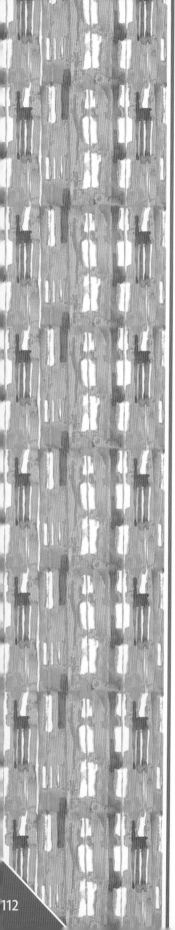

Serve over rice or lentils.

curried cauliflower

SERVES 4

2 tablespoons olive oil or ghee (clarified butter)

1 medium onion, diced

2 cloves garlic, chopped

2 small tomatoes, diced (about 1 cup)

1 teaspoon curry powder

1 teaspoon ground coriander

½ teaspoon ground turmeric

2 tablespoons chopped fresh cilantro

1 head cauliflower, cored and chopped

1 ½ cups water

salt and pepper to taste

Heat oil in a large saucepan over medium heat. Cook onions until translucent, then stir in garlic and tomatoes. Stir in curry powder, coriander, turmeric, and cilantro and bring to a simmer. Stir in cauliflower and water and continue cooking for 10 to 15 minutes, until cauliflower is tender. Season with salt and pepper.

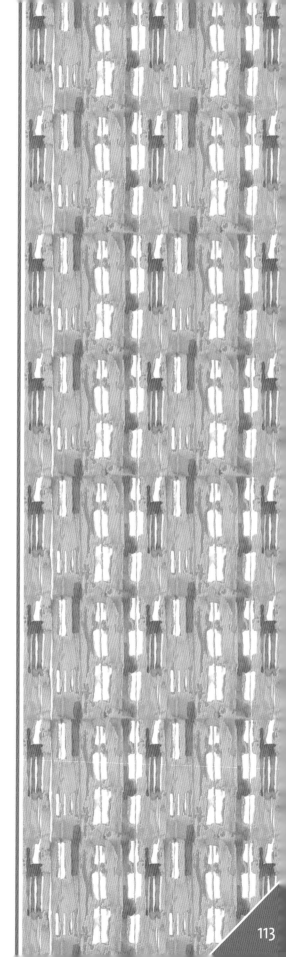

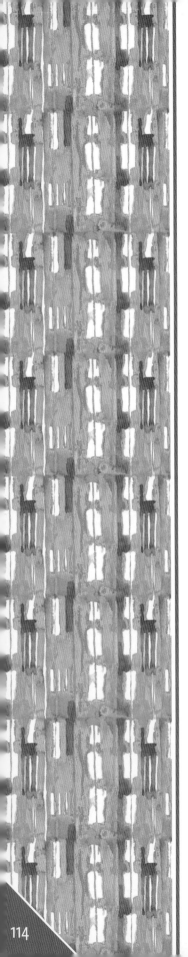

maraq baamiye

OKRA SAUCE; SERVES 6 AS A SIDE

¼ cup olive oil

½ teaspoon mustard seeds

1 onion, diced

1 teaspoon minced garlic

2 green chiles or 1 teaspoon red chile powder, optional

1 teaspoon ground cumin

1 teaspoon ground coriander

1 teaspoon ground turmeric

¼ teaspoon salt

1 tablespoon tomato paste

1 tablespoon tamarind paste or lemon juice

2 cups frozen or fresh okra, rinsed and sliced

2 large tomatoes, diced (about 2 cups)

1 teaspoon sugar

small bunch fresh cilantro

handful fresh fenugreek leaves, optional

Heat oil in a large skillet and toast mustard seeds. As soon as they start to pop, add onions, garlic, chiles, cumin, coriander, turmeric, and salt; cook 1 minute. Stir in tomato paste, tamarind, okra, tomatoes, and sugar. Cook for about 20 minutes, stirring occasionally, until the okra is tender and the pan is nearly dry. Stir in fresh herbs. Add ¼ cup water for a moist sauce.

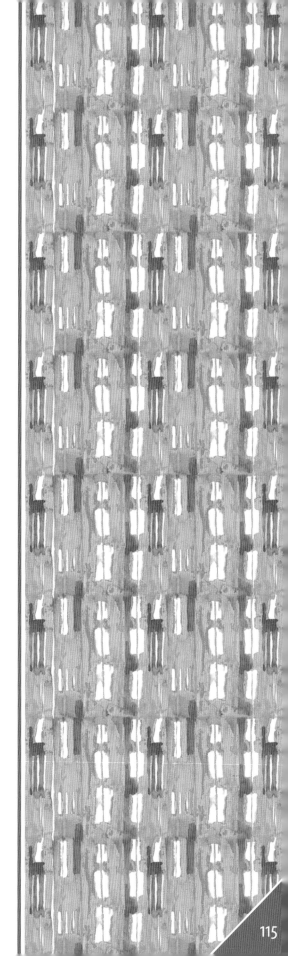

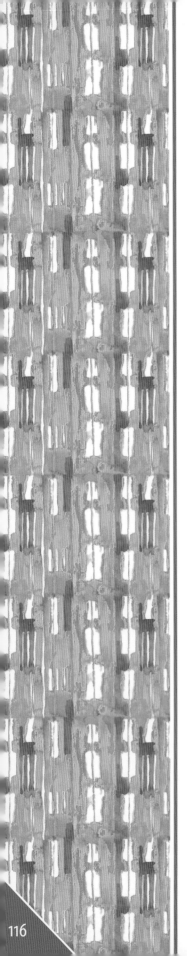

This recipe resulted when someone forgot to add potatoes to a stew. Hoda whipped up a batch of fries so nothing would go to waste.

french fries

SERVES 4

canola oil

3 russet potatoes, peeled and cut into strips

2 teaspoons ground cumin

1 teaspoon ground turmeric

1 teaspoon chile powder or to taste

1 teaspoon salt

In a large skillet, heat 1 inch oil to 300 degrees. Working in batches, add potato strips and fry until golden, about 7 to 8 minutes. Remove from oil and drain on paper towel. Repeat with remaining potatoes. Stir together cumin, turmeric, chile powder, and salt and sprinkle over fries.

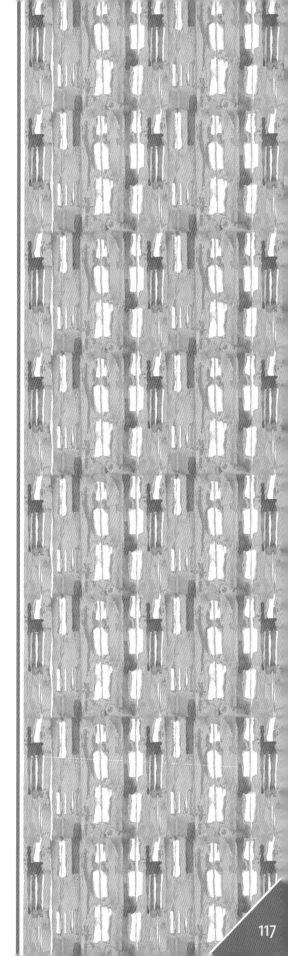

somali shidni

CHUTNEY; MAKES ABOUT 1 CUP

3 tablespoons tamarind paste

3 tomatoes, diced (about 2 cups)

2 serrano chiles*

2–3 cloves garlic

¼ cup water

¼ teaspoon salt

1 tablespoon olive oil

Combine tamarind paste, tomatoes, chiles, garlic, water, and salt in the bowl of a food processor and blend well. Heat oil in a small saucepan, add blended mixture, and cook for about 5 minutes.

⟨ *Waxannu barannay* ⟩ **WE LEARNED**

*The original recipe called for six (six!) serrano chiles. Asha commented that the serrano chiles looked three times as big as the ones she used back home. When she trusted the recipe and used all six, most people refused to even taste it. Those who tried it—well, let's just say that there wasn't a dry eye in the room that day. Here's a tip: If the sauce winds up too spicy for your liking, blend in some sugar to cut the heat.

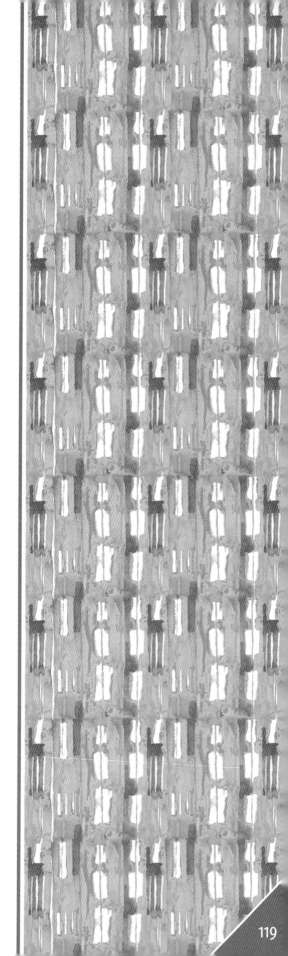

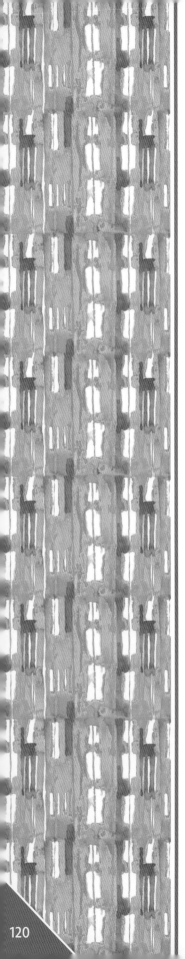

Hot sauce is a staple ingredient when eating Somali style,
but this recipe is for our less-spice-tolerant neighbors.

basbaas

MILD HOT SAUCE; MAKES ABOUT 1 CUP

2 jalapeño chiles, stemmed and seeded

1 clove garlic

1 small onion, diced

1 tomato, diced (about ¾ cup)

1 cup chopped fresh cilantro

1 teaspoon salt

¼ teaspoon pepper

juice of 1 lemon

¼ cup white vinegar

2 tablespoons canola oil

Place all ingredients in bowl of a blender and blend until smooth.
Sauce will keep in the refrigerator for up to 1 week.

rice

Somalia is bounded to the north and the east by the Indian Ocean and the Red Sea. These two bodies of water were central points of contact for Somali merchants and Asian or Middle Eastern traders as they exchanged rice, frankincense, myrrh, cinnamon, and other spices.

Bariis (rice) is a staple of Somali cuisine, accompanying suqaar and many other meat or vegetarian dishes. When it comes to cooking bariis, variations abound as assorted spices give an aromatic flair. Bariis is commonly served in a huge bowl so families can eat together.

wariyaa's bariis

SERVES 8–10

1 tablespoon olive oil

1 small onion, chopped*

1 teaspoon ground turmeric

1 teaspoon ground coriander

1 teaspoon ground cumin

¼ teaspoon salt

4 ½ cups water

3 cups basmati rice, rinsed

2 tomatoes, diced (about 1 ½ cups)

handful chopped fresh cilantro

Heat oil in a large skillet and add onions, turmeric, coriander, cumin, and salt, stirring to combine. Cook over medium heat for 5 minutes or until onions are softened. In a large pan or rice cooker, stir together water, rice, tomatoes, and onion mixture. Bring to a boil, then reduce heat to low and cook, covered, for 20 minutes or until rice reaches desired texture. Top with cilantro.

⟨ *Waxannu barannay* ⟩ WE LEARNED

One day, we forgot the onion and Asha got upset. "You always put an onion in rice," she said. The Wariyaa instructor's response was, "Then you have to put it in the recipe! How else am I going to know?" From then on, an extra onion was always added for good measure.

Whose rice is better than your family's recipe?
Successfully making rice "just like Mom's" was
the ultimate complement to our meals.

mom's home rice*

SERVES 8–10

7 chicken bouillon cubes

5–7 tablespoons vegetable or olive oil

½ white onion, chopped

3 cloves garlic, minced

2 cinnamon sticks

1 teaspoon curry powder

1 teaspoon ground cloves

1 teaspoon onion salt

¼ teaspoon salt

2 medium tomatoes, diced (about 1 ½ cups)

3 cups basmati rice, rinsed

1 bunch fresh cilantro, minced, optional

Heat oven to 400 degrees. Bring 6 cups water to near boiling
and add bouillon cubes, stirring to dissolve. Set aside. In a deep,
oven-safe pan with a lid, warm vegetable oil over medium heat
and cook onions, garlic, cinnamon sticks, curry powder, cloves,
onion salt, and salt until onions are softened. Add tomatoes and
cook, stirring, for 3 to 5 minutes. Pour warm broth into the pan
and stir in rice. Cover pan and bake 30 to 45 minutes, checking
for texture and adding more water as needed. Garnish with
cilantro (if using).

⟨ *Waxannu barannay* ⟩ WE LEARNED

*Hamdi followed her mom around the kitchen
to gather the directions for this dish.

Turmeric is a common addition to many Somali and African dishes. Turmeric rice is a simple and delicious accompaniment to any curry or as a side dish for lunch or dinner.

bariis xawaash leh

TURMERIC RICE; SERVES 8+

1 tablespoon olive oil

2 tablespoons subag (ghee or clarified butter)

3 cups basmati rice, rinsed

1 teaspoon ground turmeric

1 teaspoon ground coriander

1 teaspoon ground cumin

¼ teaspoon salt

handful chopped fresh cilantro

4 ½ cups water

Heat oven to 225 degrees. Heat olive oil and subag in a saucepan over medium heat and stir-fry the rice for 2 minutes, until dry. Stir in the turmeric, coriander, cumin, salt, and cilantro. Add the water, reduce heat to low, and cook, covered, until the rice absorbs the liquid, about 20 minutes. Remove pan from heat, replace lid with aluminum foil, and place in oven for 5 minutes* to drive off any excess moisture.

⟨ *Waxannu barannay* ⟩ WE LEARNED

The students used large bowls to rinse the rice, pouring hot water back and forth between them. An Asian American staff member, unaccustomed to this practice, looked a little horrified at first, but soon came around to this approach.

*We often omitted this step to save time, but Hamze commented that it made the difference between the flavor and texture of an amateur's rice and his grandma's.

brown rice pilaf
SERVES 6–8

2 tablespoons coconut oil or vegetable oil

1 onion, chopped

8–10 cardamom pods

1 teaspoon fenugreek seeds

1 teaspoon coriander seeds

2 cups brown rice

1 tablespoon ground cumin

1 tablespoon ground turmeric

5 whole black peppercorns

¼ teaspoon salt

1 cup cubed sweet potato, pumpkin, or carrot

2 tablespoons chopped fresh cilantro

2 tablespoons sultanas or raisins, optional

Bring 4 cups water to boiling. Heat oil in large saucepan over medium heat and cook onions until translucent. Add cardamom pods, fenugreek seeds, and coriander seeds, toasting to deepen flavor. (Alternatively, toast spices on a baking sheet in the oven or in a dry pan on the stovetop for 5 minutes to deepen the flavor.) Stir in rice, cumin, turmeric, and peppercorns. Add boiling water and salt; cover and cook for about 5 minutes. Stir in sweet potato, cilantro, and sultanas (if using); reduce heat to low and cook, covered, for about 30 minutes, checking frequently and adding more water as needed. Remove from heat and set aside, covered, for 10 minutes to yield a slightly chewy texture.

bariis iskukaris
AROMATIC RICE; SERVES 10–12

4 cups basmati rice, rinsed

½ cup olive oil

1 large yellow onion, chopped

3 cloves garlic, minced

2 cinnamon sticks

5 green cardamom pods

10 whole cloves

2 teaspoons Xawaash (page 142)

8 cups chicken stock

1 teaspoon saffron threads, minced

1 cup raisins

salt

FOR THE TOPPING

2 tablespoons olive oil

1 red onion, thinly sliced

¼ cup raisins

1 red bell pepper, cored and thinly sliced

salt

Soak rice in cold water for 30 to 45 minutes; drain.

Prepare the topping: Heat 2 tablespoons olive oil in a wide, deep pot over medium-high heat and cook red onions, stirring occasionally, until translucent. Stir in raisins and allow to soften, about 2 minutes. Stir in red bell pepper and cook until softened, about 5 to 7 minutes. Season with salt and scoop mixture onto a paper towel to drain.

In the same pot, make the rice: Heat ½ cup olive oil and cook yellow onions, stirring frequently, until softened, 6 to 8 minutes. Add garlic, cinnamon sticks, cardamom, cloves, and xawaash; stir for about 1 minute. Stir in stock and rice. Bring to boil, then cover and cook on low heat for 20 minutes. Stir in saffron and raisins and season with salt to taste. Remove from heat and set aside, covered, for 5 minutes. Heap rice on a serving platter, sprinkle with topping, and serve.

bariis surbiyaan

SPICY RICE WITH CARAMELIZED ONIONS; SERVES 6

3 tablespoons olive oil, divided

1 large onion cut into thin strips

2 teaspoons ground cardamom

1 teaspoon ground cinnamon

1 teaspoon ground cumin

½ jalapeño chile, seeded and diced

3 cloves garlic, minced

2 tablespoons chopped fresh cilantro

2 cups basmati rice, rinsed

1 chicken bouillon cube (omit for vegetarian dish)

Heat 2 tablespoons oil in skillet over low heat and slowly cook
onions until browned and caramelized, about 15 minutes.
Set aside.

In a large saucepan, heat remaining 1 tablespoon oil and cook
cardamom, cinnamon, cumin, jalapeño, garlic, and cilantro
until jalapeño has softened. Add rice, bouillon cube, and water
to cover rice by 3 inches (approximately 4 cups). Bring to a boil,
reduce heat to low, cover, and cook until rice is tender, about
15 to 20 minutes. Serve topped with caramelized onions.

This delicious rice dish, with its hearty components of tomatoes, beans or lentils, and herbs, is commonly served with sesame oil and a sprinkling of sugar. It may also be topped with fried onions.

cambuulo iyo maraq
SPICY BEANS; SERVES 4

1 cup long-grain basmati rice, rinsed

salt

1 cup cooked adzuki beans or any kind of lentil*

2 tablespoons sesame oil

1 large onion, diced

2 cloves garlic, minced

2 tablespoons tomato paste

1 teaspoon chile powder or chile flakes, or 2 green chiles, diced

1 teaspoon ground coriander

1 teaspoon ground cumin

1 (14.5-ounce) can diced tomatoes,
or 6 tomatoes, diced, some reserved for garnish

1 tablespoon white vinegar

juice of 1 lemon

toasted almonds and fresh cilantro for garnish

In a medium saucepan, combine rice with 1 ½ cups water and a pinch of salt. Cook, covered, over low heat until the rice is tender, about 15 minutes. Stir in the beans and set aside.

Heat sesame oil in a skillet and cook onions until translucent. Stir in the garlic and cook for about 1 minute. Stir in tomato paste, chile, coriander, and cumin and cook, stirring, 1 minute. Add tomatoes and cook for about 5 minutes. Add water as needed to maintain a thick, soupy consistency. Stir in vinegar and lemon juice and simmer over low heat for about 5 minutes.

Serve rice-lentil mixture in a bowl topped with tomato sauce. Garnish with diced tomato, toasted nuts, or fresh cilantro.

⟨ *Waxannu barannay* ⟩ WE LEARNED

*Or use dried beans: soak overnight, drain, cover with water, and boil for 20 minutes.

vegetable risotto

SERVES 4–6

2 tablespoons butter

1 onion, chopped

2 cups chopped summer squash and zucchini, optional

5–6 mushrooms, chopped

2 cups Arborio rice

6 cups warm vegetable stock, divided

salt and pepper

1 teaspoon grated lemon or lime zest

½ cup grated Parmesan cheese, plus more for serving

Heat butter in large saucepan over medium heat and add onions, cooking slowly until browned and caramelized. Add mixed vegetables (if using) and mushrooms and cook, stirring occasionally, for about 4 minutes. Add rice and cook, stirring, for several minutes, until the rice is transparent. Slowly add in 1 cup stock and continue cooking and stirring until the stock is nearly absorbed. Repeat with additional stock, 1 cup at a time, until 4 cups of stock have been absorbed. Add the remaining 2 cups of stock and cook and stir another 5 minutes or so, until rice is al dente. If the rice seems dry, add a bit of water. Stir in a pinch of salt, a pinch of pepper, lemon or lime zest, and Parmesan cheese. Serve, sprinkled with more Parmesan cheese.

Somali households often make a large batch of this spice blend to last the month or longer. Most often used to flavor rice, it adds a taste of home to meat dishes as well.

xawaash
SOMALI SPICE MIX; MAKES 1/3 CUP

1 tablespoon cumin seeds

1 tablespoon coriander seeds

2 teaspoons dried sage leaves

1 teaspoon black peppercorns

1 teaspoon fenugreek seeds

1 teaspoon ground turmeric

1 ¼ teaspoons ground ginger

8 green cardamom pods

10 whole cloves

¼ teaspoon freshly grated nutmeg

⅓ cinnamon stick

Combine all ingredients and grind with a food processor, coffee mill, or mortar and pestle until smooth.

6

drinks

Beverages accompany Somali social activity. Since Somalis are Muslim and do not consume alcohol, *shaah* (tea) is central to family gatherings or meetings with friends to discuss worldly affairs. Traditional Somali drinks also consist of a variety of tropical flavors: watermelon, mango, banana, pomegranate, grapefruit, and guava. Smoothies are commonly paired with spicy meals to help tame the heat.

A family member suggested that Hoda stop drinking milky teas as they would make her gain weight. Do you have a family member who would suggest that? She decided to make her own choices and still enjoys her tea.

This tea allows for customization: add milk and sugar as desired. It can also be served as an iced tea in the summer.

shaah

SOMALI TEA; SERVES 6

5 cups water

6–7 black tea bags

2 tablespoons freshly grated ginger

2–3 whole cloves, crushed

5 cardamom pods, crushed

1 cinnamon stick

½ teaspoon ground nutmeg

milk and sugar

In a large saucepan, bring water to a boil. Add tea bags and spices (ginger, cloves, cardamom, cinnamon, nutmeg) and boil for 30 minutes. Drain through a strainer to remove spices. Serve with milk and sugar to taste.

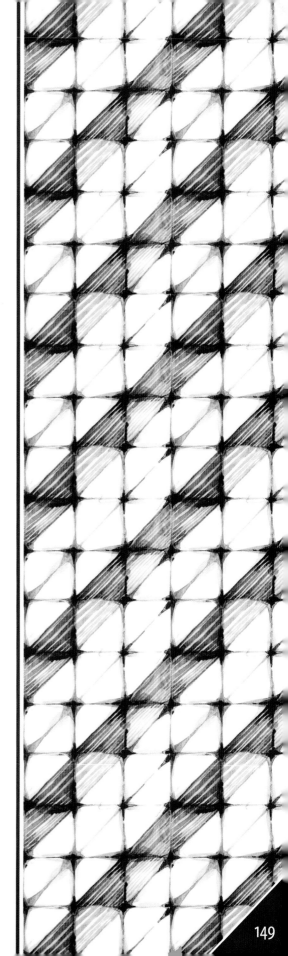

"I started drinking shaah cadays because my mom forced me into drinking it. I always had [an] interest in [the] tea that she was making so I snuck into the kitchen one day and drank it. I burned my tongue and I started running around crying, so instead of drinking tea my mom introduced me to shaah cadays. I've been drinking it ever since until I was twelve."—Abdirahman

This tea is a wonderfully warming winter beverage. Remove the tea bags or tea leaves sooner for a lighter, milder tea.

shaah cadays ah
SOMALI TEA WITH MILK; MAKES 4 CUPS

10 cardamom pods

5 whole cloves

4 black peppercorns

2 cinnamon sticks, broken in half

2 cups water

2 cups whole milk

1 cup sugar

4 tea bags or 2 tablespoons black tea leaves

Place cardamom pods, cloves, peppercorns, and cinnamon sticks in a tea bag or a tea ball. In a saucepan over medium heat, combine the water, milk, sugar, and spices and bring to a boil. Add the tea and steep on low heat for 5 to 10 minutes. Remove tea bags and spices or drain through a strainer and serve.

⟨ *Waxannu barannay* ⟩ **WE LEARNED**

Lacking tea bags or a tea ball, we smashed the cardamom pods to open them up and tossed in the rest of the spices whole. We strained the tea before drinking.

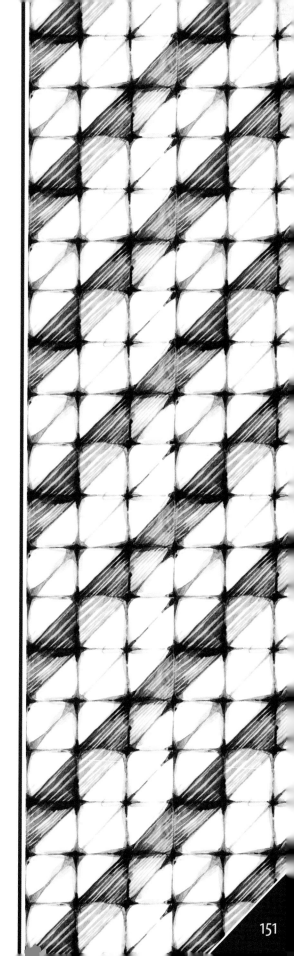

Coffee shops offer a cultural center for Somali elders to meet. In Minneapolis's Cedar-Riverside area, coffee shops bustle with talk of Somali and American politics, conversations to share, and plenty of coffee to enjoy. We predict this recipe will rival the offerings at your local coffee shop.

qaxwo
COFFEE; SERVES 4

2 cups whole milk

7 cardamom pods

2 cinnamon sticks

2 tablespoons sugar

2 tablespoons freshly ground coffee

Bring milk to a boil in a saucepan over medium heat. Crush the cardamom and cinnamon using a mortar and pestle. Add the cardamom, cinnamon, sugar, and coffee to the milk. Reduce heat to low and steep for 3 to 4 minutes. Strain and serve.

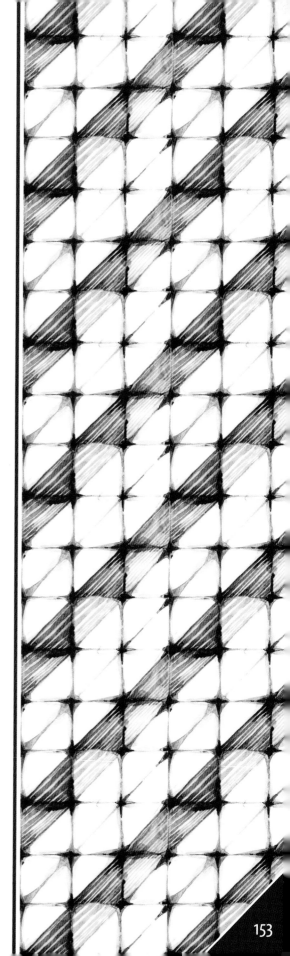

Pineapple is a common dessert ingredient; the juice makes a popular drink that is sweet and refreshing.

cananaas cabbid ah

PINEAPPLE JUICE; SERVES 3

1 ½ cups water, divided

½ cup sugar

1 pineapple, peeled, cored, and cut into chunks

ice cubes

In a small saucepan over medium heat, heat ½ cup water and sugar for about 4 minutes, stirring until sugar dissolves. Set aside to cool.

Combine the pineapple chunks and remaining 1 cup water in bowl of a blender; blend until smooth. Blend in the syrup to taste. Pour the juice over ice and stir well before serving.

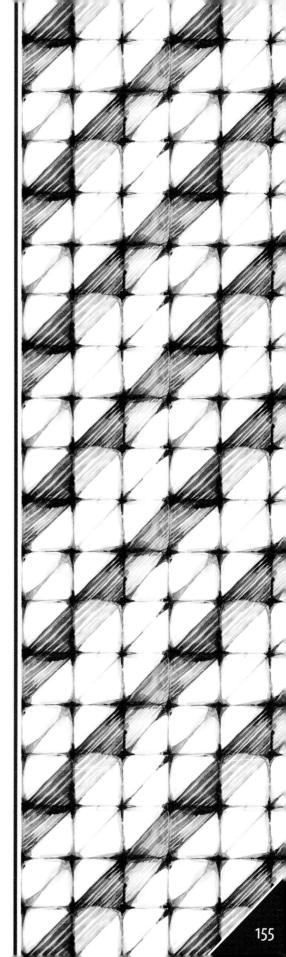

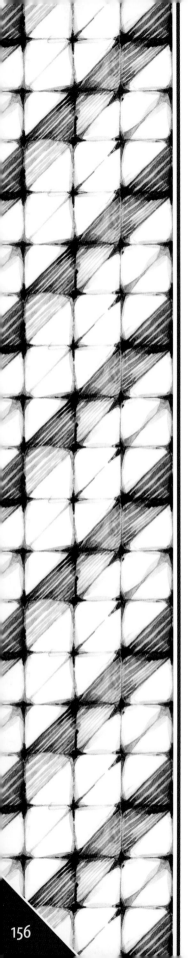

"I remember when I was a kid and I used to follow my dad to his restaurant, I always used to get mango juice for free. And when I came to America, I used to get it because I couldn't drink tea or coffee yet." —Abdirahman

Mango juice, light and refreshing, is a popular summer drink in Somalia.

biyo cambe
MANGO JUICE; SERVES 4

2 cups peeled, chopped ripe mango

1 cup milk

1 cup plain yogurt

sugar to taste

Combine all ingredients in bowl of a blender and blend until smooth. Add a little water to thin if necessary.

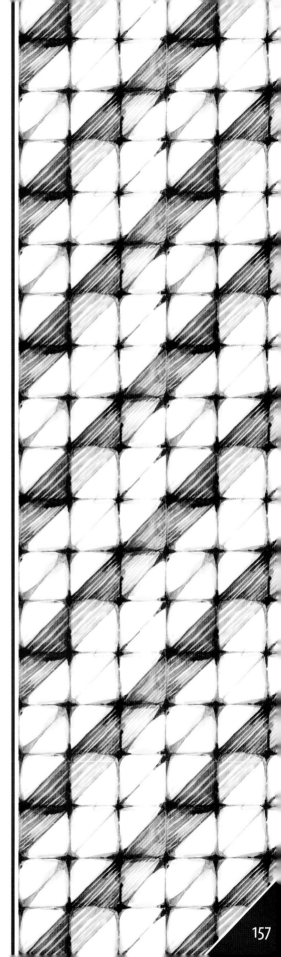

desserts

Mac macaan is the Somali word for desserts, served after meals and at special gatherings and celebrations. Somali nomads sweetened their food with dates, sorghum, sugar, or honey, accompanied by a cup of hot shaah. Kashata, kakkac, and xalwo are just a few of many Somali treats. Xalwo in particular brings a smile to kids' faces.

Popular in northern Africa and inspired by Middle Eastern traditions, this dessert can be served with a favorite citrus or simple syrup.

semolina cake

SERVES 12

2 cups water, divided

4 ½ cups sugar, divided

juice of ½ lemon, lime, or orange

½ cup vegetable oil or softened butter (1 stick)

3 tablespoons milk

3 eggs

2 cups semolina flour

2 teaspoons baking powder

Preheat oven to 350 degrees and grease a 9-inch square pan. In a small saucepan, heat 1 cup water and 3 cups sugar with citrus juice. Bring to boiling and cook for 5 minutes. Remove from heat and set aside.

In a bowl, beat together the oil, remaining 1 ½ cups sugar, remaining 1 cup water, and milk until creamy. Beat in the eggs one at a time. Stir in the semolina and baking powder until combined. Pour into the prepared pan and level the top. Bake for 30 minutes or until golden.

Cut the cake into squares or diamonds, then pour the cooled syrup over the hot cake. Let cool in the pan before serving.

Baking was new for everyone. Some of us thought this cake would be the easy assignment. Now we appreciate our mom's baking all the more. Through a friendly competition in the kitchen, we reached this verdict: we're all winners!

doolsho / keeg

VANILLA CAKE; SERVES 12

1 cup sugar

3 eggs

1 ½ cups all-purpose flour

2 teaspoons baking powder

½ teaspoon salt

1 teaspoon ground cardamom

½ teaspoon vanilla extract

½ cup vegetable oil

½ cup whole milk

confectioner's sugar, optional

Preheat oven to 350 degrees and grease a 9-inch square pan. Mix sugar and eggs together until well combined. Stir in flour, baking powder, salt, cardamom, vanilla, oil, and milk, mixing until smooth. Pour batter into prepared pan and bake for 30 to 40 minutes, until golden brown and a wooden pick inserted at the center comes out clean. Sprinkle confectioner's sugar over top if desired.

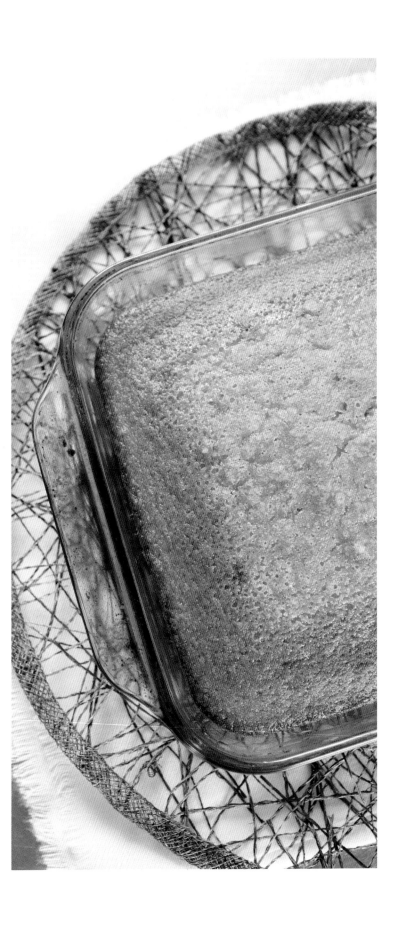

mahamri
AFRICAN DONUTS; MAKES 32 SMALL DONUTS

1 tablespoon instant yeast

3 cups all-purpose flour

½ cup sugar

1 teaspoon ground cardamom

1 cup coconut milk powder plus ¾ cup warm milk, or substitute 1 (14-ounce) can coconut milk

canola oil for frying

Mix the yeast into ¼ cup warm water; stir in a pinch of flour and a pinch of sugar. Set aside until bubbly.

In a large bowl, stir together the flour, sugar, cardamom, coconut powder, warm milk, and yeast mixture, kneading to form a smooth dough. Let the dough rest in a warm place, preferably overnight, until double in size.

Divide dough into 8 balls. Roll each ball into a 6-inch circle and cut into quarters. Pour oil in a deep skillet set over medium heat, and heat to 375 degrees. Drop 3 to 4 triangles into the hot oil; the dough should quickly float to the top and puff up. As soon as mahamri are a light brown, turn and cook on the other side for another minute, until light golden brown. Remove from oil with a slotted spoon and drain on a paper towel–lined plate.

While many people see an Italian influence in these donuts, this dish is truly Somali. These were a fun afternoon treat, even if we had to wait for the world's slowest deep fryer to warm up.

kackac
SOMALI BEIGNETS; SERVES 10

2 cups all-purpose flour

½ cup granulated sugar

1 teaspoon baking powder

2 eggs

8 tablespoons (1 stick) unsalted butter, melted

2 tablespoons warm milk

canola oil for frying

confectioner's sugar, maple sugar, or honey for serving

In a large bowl, stir together flour, granulated sugar, and baking powder, mixing well. Add eggs, melted butter, and warm milk and mix well. Knead on a floured surface for 3 minutes. Let the dough rest for 10 minutes. Roll out the dough to ¼ inch thick. Cut into 24 pieces. Roll into balls. Heat oil to 375 degrees and fry kackac a few at a time for 3 to 4 minutes, until golden brown. Drain on a paper towel–lined plate. Dust with sifted confectioner's or maple sugar if desired or serve with honey.

〈 *Waxannu barannay* 〉 WE LEARNED

The traditional method calls for square beignets, but our group liked to make them round, like donut holes.

Named for the pattern of the finished dish, honeycomb bread has become a new staple for dessert. Be creative: choose among any of several fillings, and surprise your friends and family with what's inside.

rooti malab

HONEYCOMB BREAD; MAKES 32 BALLS

⅔ cup warm milk, plus more for brushing

2 teaspoons instant yeast

3 tablespoons plus 1 teaspoon sugar, divided

2 cups all-purpose flour

¼ teaspoon salt

¼ teaspoon baking powder

3 tablespoons butter, melted

6 ounces cream cheese

dates, peanut butter, fruit, raisins, coconut, or chocolate chips for filling, optional

1 (14-ounce) can sweetened condensed milk, optional

Heat oven to 375 degrees and grease a 9x13–inch pan. In a small bowl, stir together ⅔ cup warm milk, yeast, and 1 teaspoon sugar. Set aside for 10 minutes, until bubbly. In a large bowl, stir together flour, remaining 3 tablespoons sugar, salt, baking powder, and melted butter, then stir in the yeast mixture. Knead dough on a floured surface for 5 minutes, adding water if needed to create an elastic dough. Cover the bowl with a damp towel and let dough rise for 1 hour.

Divide dough into approximately 32 equal pieces and form into balls. Flatten each dough piece with your fingers, then place a scant teaspoon cream cheese plus other fillings as desired on it. Pinch the dough closed around the filling, and then roll into a ball. Place the dough balls in prepared pan, spacing them evenly. Brush tops with milk. Bake for 20 minutes. Pour condensed milk over top if desired, then scoop out of pan to serve.

This delicious dessert has roots in the Dutch *aebleskiver*. If you do not have the specialized pan, use a cast-iron muffin tin instead.

macsharo yariis
MINI RICE AND COCONUT CAKES; SERVES 10

2 cups basmati rice, soaked overnight and drained

¾ cup coconut powder

¾ cup sugar

1 tablespoon instant yeast

2 teaspoons all-purpose flour, optional

¼ teaspoon ground cardamom

1–1 ¼ cups warm milk

canola oil for cooking

In a large bowl, combine rice, coconut powder, sugar, yeast, flour (if using), cardamom, and milk, blending until smooth and the consistency of pancake batter. Add ¼ cup water if the mixture seems too thick. Set aside until doubled in size, about 1 hour.

Brush oil over an aebleskiver pan and place over medium heat. Use a spoon to pour the mixture into each compartment, filling to the top. Reduce heat to low. When the tops are bubbly and the bottoms are brown, use a skewer or wooden pick to flip and cook the other side. When both sides are browned, remove to a platter. Continue with remaining batter.

173

The entire class enjoyed making this candy, especially Asha. Her sweet tooth often got the better of her: she couldn't wait until it dried into balls and could be found about to taste a whole spoonful!

kashata

COCONUT CANDY; SERVES 10+

1 ½ cups desiccated (dried and shredded) coconut or fresh grated coconut (about 2 small coconuts)

1 cup sugar

½ teaspoon ground cardamom

If using desiccated coconut, mix with ½ cup water and set aside. Grease a plate or baking sheet. In a large saucepan, cook sugar with ¾ cup water on low heat for about 4 minutes. Stir occasionally and watch to be sure the sugar doesn't burn. If coconut is soaking, drain. Stir coconut and cardamom into sugar mixture. Cook over low heat, stirring until well mixed and heated through.

Pour mixture onto prepared plate or baking sheet. Immediately flatten with a buttered knife and cut into desired shapes, or let cool and then shape mixture into balls.

This bread is great as a snack alongside shaah or spread with butter and enjoyed for dessert.

date & banana loaf

SERVES 8

⅓ cup unsalted butter, melted

⅓ cup sugar

2 tablespoons honey

2 eggs

3 ripe bananas

½ cup chopped dates

1 cup all-purpose flour

½ cup whole-wheat flour

1 ½ teaspoons baking powder

½ teaspoon salt

Preheat oven to 375 degrees and grease a 9x5–inch loaf pan. In a large bowl, whisk butter, sugar, and honey for 5 minutes. Add eggs one at a time, mixing until incorporated. In a food processor, purée bananas and dates. Stir into the batter. Then stir in flours, baking powder, and salt.

Spoon mixture into prepared pan and smooth top. Bake for 1 hour. Let cool 10 minutes before removing from pan.

Bananas are an important part of every Somali meal, and desserts are no exception. These fritters are often served with tea or milk as an afternoon snack.

banana fritters

SERVES 6

1 cup milk

1 egg

2 bananas, chopped

1 teaspoon vanilla

2 ½ cups all-purpose flour

3 teaspoons baking powder

¼ cup granulated sugar

pinch salt

½ teaspoon ground cardamom

½ teaspoon ground cinnamon

canola oil for frying

confectioner's sugar

Place milk, egg, bananas, vanilla, flour, baking powder, granulated sugar, salt, cardamom, and cinnamon in bowl of a stand mixer or blender and process until thick. Add more flour if the batter is too runny.

Pour oil to 1 inch deep in a pan and heat to 375 degrees. Use a slotted spoon to drop balls of dough a few at a time into the hot oil. Cook until golden brown, turning once, then drain fritters on a paper towel–lined plate. Let cool and then dust with confectioner's sugar.

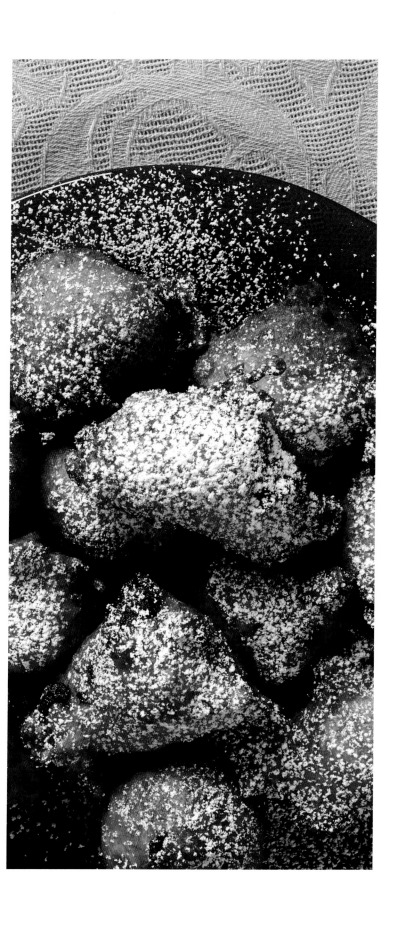

acknowledgments

The Wariyaa program was developed and facilitated by Jessica Hobson, an Inclusion and Community Engagement Specialist at the Minnesota Historical Society.

The student participants were Abidwahid Abdi, Naima Abdi, Abdikarim Aden, Hamdi Ahmed, Hamze Ahmed, Abdirahman Dirie, Asha Mohamed, Hamse Mohamed, and Hoda Musse.

Thank you to Chris Taylor and members of the Department of Inclusion and Community Engagement for their vision and support of this project.

Thank you to South High School, Minneapolis, for supporting many of our students through their first high school internship, and to the family members who shared their stories and drove us around.

This program could not have run without Wini Froelich, who opened the Mill City Museum doors, and Sarah Coleman, who made the kitchen feel like home.

Many thanks to Said Salah Ahmed for reviewing our work and correcting our spelling.

Thank you to Minnesota Historical Society interns who helped in ways large and small:

Ian Marquez
Jae Yates
Saida Mahamud
Dae Akre-Fens

Angie Vimonkhon
Neng Vue
Molly Leone
Kirsten Uhlenberg

Thank you to the cooks who contributed to our recipe-testing days and our photo shoots:

Beth Black
Allison Broughton
Joanna Danks
Weston Danks
Elena Everson
Michael Fisch
Jessica Hobson
Nancy Hoffman
Maryan Hussein
    Mohamed
Maren Gregorson
    Levad
Josh Leventhal
Anne Levin

Kaytlyn Lundstrom
Stephen Malling
Jennifer McElroy
Sam Meshbesher
Isha Mohamed
    Ahmed
Joey Novacheck
Lauren Peck
Shannon Pennefeather
Mary Poggione
Ann Regan
Laura Roller
Teri Springer
Jae Yates

And for capturing step-by-step photos of our adventures in the kitchen as well as photographing dish after dish in intense photo shoots, we are grateful to James Castle.

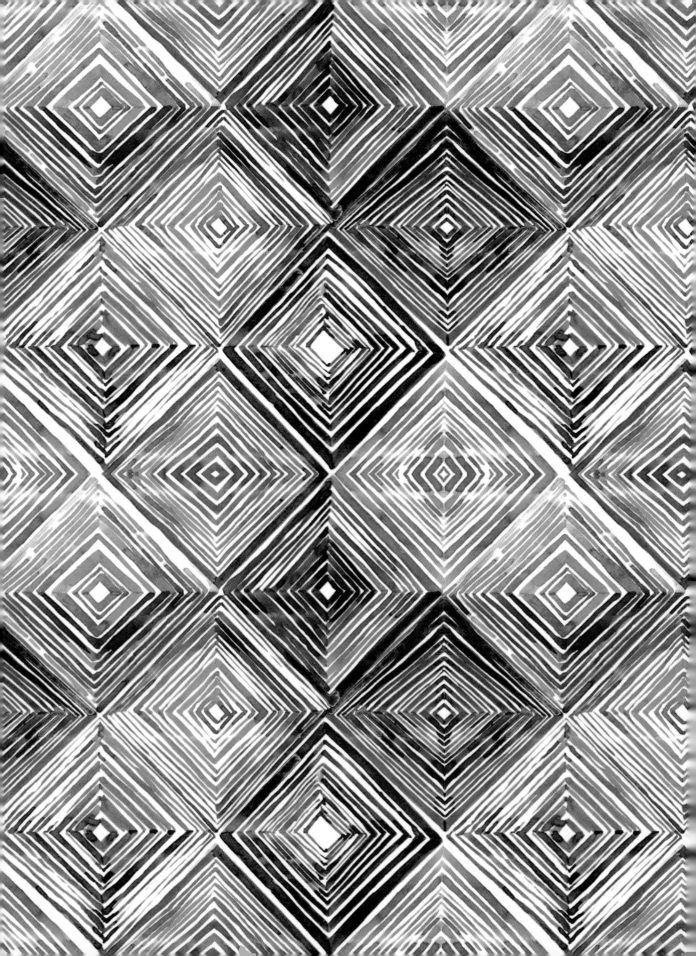

index

BUSKUD, PAGE 32

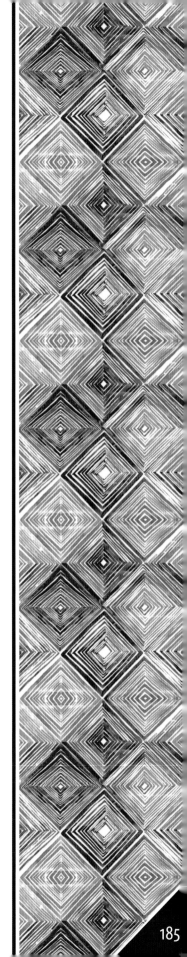

CHICKEN SUQAAR, PAGE 68

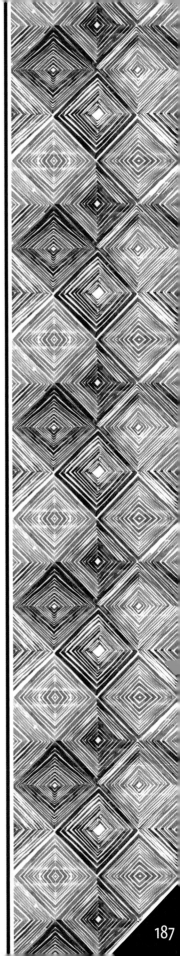

COCONUT-FILLED SABAAYAD, PAGE 54

MISHKAKI, PAGE 74

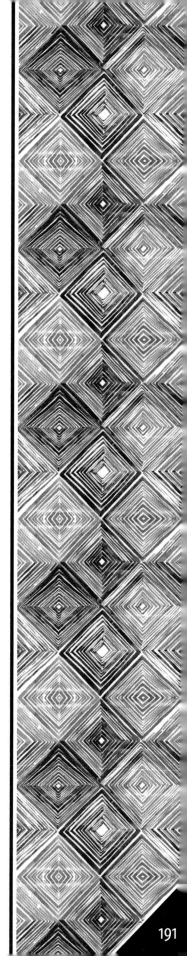

WALNUT & CUMIN LENTIL SALAD, PAGE 94

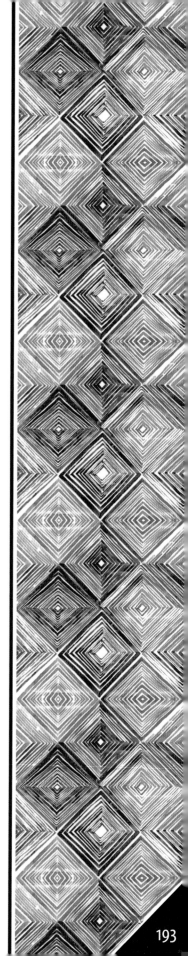

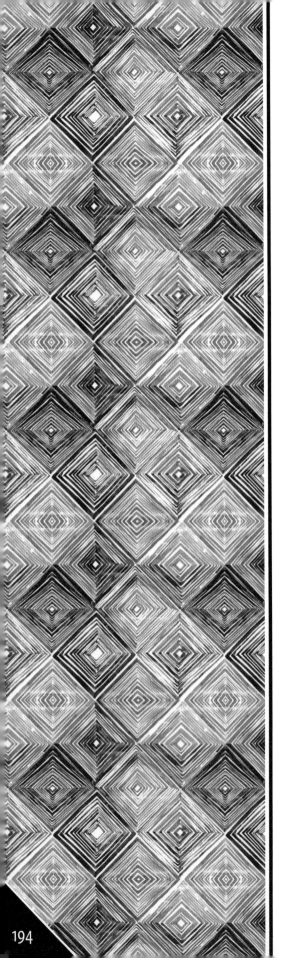

BAASTO, PAGE 78

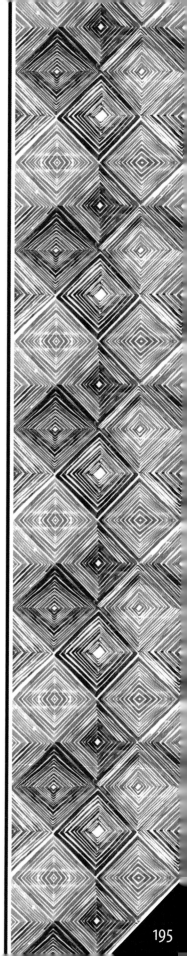

XAWAASH, PAGE 142

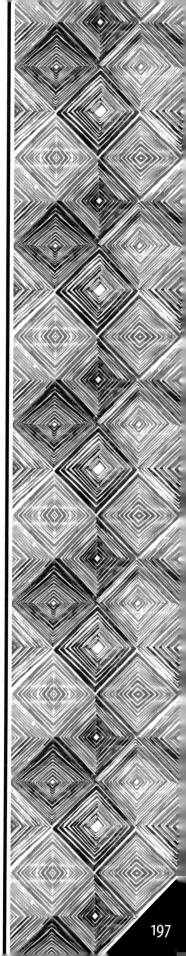

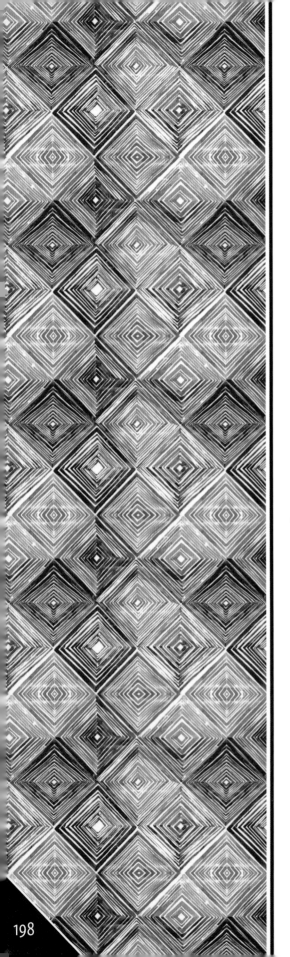

KHUDAAR LA SHIILAY, PAGE 106